CORNERSTONE UNIVERSITY
MILLER LIBRARY
1001 E. BELTLINE NE
GRAND RAPIDS, MI 49525-5897

IGOR STRAVINSKY

Pribaoutki, Renard and Ragtime for Eleven Instruments

DOVER PUBLICATIONS, INC.
Mineola, New York

Copyright

Bibliographical Note

This Dover edition, first published in 2000, is a new compilation of three works originally published separately.

Pribaoutki (Chansons Plaisantes) for Medium Voice and 8 Instruments and *Renard: Histoire burlesque chantée et jouée* (this title also appears in Russian and German) were originally published separately by Ad. Henn, Geneva/J. & W. Chester, Ltd. (Chester Music), London, 1917. *Ragtime for Eleven Instruments* was originally published by Editions de la Sirène, Paris, 1919, and reprinted by Chester Music (Chester Music Limited), London, 1920.

All prefatory sections were specially prepared for this edition, including a glossary of French musical terms in the three scores and Stanley Appelbaum's notes and text translations for both *Pribaoutki* and *Renard*. The note for *Ragtime* was largely adapted from Eric Walter White's *Stravinsky: A Critical Survey, 1882–1946* (Dover, 1997).

International Standard Book Number: 0-486-41395-0

Manufactured in the United States of America
Dover Publications, Inc., 31 East 2nd Street, Mineola, N.Y. 11501

CONTENTS

GLOSSARY OF FRENCH TERMS IN THE SCORES

à grelots, with jingles [tambourine]
au talon, at the heel [of the bow]
avec (2) doigts, with (2) fingers
avec grelots, with jingles [tambourine]
avec le pouce, thumb roll [tambourine]
avec toute la longueur de l'archet, with the full length of the bow

bag(uette), stick, beater [percussion]
(à tête) en capoc [kapok], with a medium-soft cushioned head
en bois, wooden snare drum stick
en cuir, with a hide-covered head
en éponge, with a soft ("sponge") head
en feutre (dur), with a (hard) felt-covered head
en jonc, with a stiff cane shaft
bois, wood (shaft of a beater); *les bois*, woodwinds
bouché, "stopped" sound [horn]

coup de genou(x), struck on the knee(s) [tambourine]
court, short
cuivré, brassy
cuivrez, play with a resounding sound
cymbale contre cymbale, cymbal against cymbal

de la m(ain) d(roite), with the right hand
de la m(ain) g(auche), with the left hand
de la membrane, of the drumhead
du talon, from the heel [of the bow]

enchaînez = segue
en dehors, distant
en glissant le doigt, while sliding the finger
environ, approximately [tempo]
et, and
étouffez, "choked" [cut-off sound]

fin(e), end

gliss(ando) pour la timb(ale) à levier, *glissando* for the pedal timpani

jeté, bounced, "thrown" bowing

laissez vibrer, let it sound

mailloche, bass drum beater
m(ain) d(roite), right hand
m(ain) g(auche), left hand

ordinairement, in the usual way
ouvert, open

préparez vite, quickly prepare
près du chevalet [also, *tout près*], near [quite near] the bridge [cimbalom]

sans grelots, without jingles [tambourine]
sec, dry, abrupt

talon, heel [of the bow]
tout l'archet, full bow
très court (et mordant), very short (and biting)
très détaché, very detached
très sec, very dry, abrupt

FOOTNOTES AND LONGER SCORE NOTES

Page 28, footnote (for Cimbalom):
Les notes marqués du signe "o" se jouent derrière le chevalet de l'instrument
The notes marked "o" are to be played behind the bridge of the instrument

Page 46, footnote (for Tenor II):
Prononcez: confessère
Pronounce [confesser]: confessère

Page 59, footnote (for Cimbalom):
Pour l'instrument qui a le ré grave exécuter . . .
For an instrument with the low D, play . . .
[Similar footnotes appear on pp. 60, 61, 79, 110, 111, 112, 128, 129 and 194.]

Page 73, footnote (for Tenor I):
Note basse indeterminée
Indefinite low pitch

Page 75, 2nd bar, Cimbalom:
ouvrez peu à peu la pédale
open [depress] the pedal little by little
[reoccurs on p. 93, 1st bar]

Page 96, footnotes (for Bass I, Tenor I):
[For the Russian text, sing the phrase as shown.]
Pour le français et l'allemand cette fin de la phrase est confiée au 1er ténor, la basse se taisant.
For the French and German texts, this phrase ending is for Tenor I only, Bass I remaining silent.

Page 123, footnote (for Cimbalom, Cello, Bass and Timpani):
Pour l'instrument qui a le ré grave, exécuter . . .
Supprimez dans ce cas les parties des Violoncelle, Contrabasse et timbales du [63]:
For [a cimbalom] with the low D, play . . . [*example*]
In this case, omit the cello, bass and timpani parts from [63]:
[continues through pp. 124–5, then again at p. 133]

Page 130, footnote (for Cimbalom and Timpani):
En cas que le ré grave du Cimbalum [sic] *manque remplacez-le par la timbale*
If the cimbalom's low D is missing, let the timpani play that note.
[continues through pp. 131–3]

Page 141, footnote (for Bass I):
The Russian note says: "The transition from the *yeh*-sound to the *oo*-sound should be sudden. The *oo*-sound should be pronounced with the lips, imitating the sound of the lowest string on the bass."
[reoccurs on p. 145]

Page 150, footnote (for Cimbalom and Bass):
Ces notes mises entre parenthèse se jouent seulement au cas où le Cimbalum ne possède pas le ré grave.
Play the parenthetical notes [in the bass part] only if the cimbalom lacks a low D.
[continues through pp. 151, 155, 158, 159, 164, 165 and 169]

Page 192, footnote (for Side Drum):
Les queues en bas—m.g. avec la mailloche
Les queues en haut—m.d. bag. en capoc
Downstemmed notes—left hand with the bass drum beater.
Upstemmed notes—right hand with a beater with a medium-soft cushioned head.

To my wife

Pribaoutki

(Nonsense Rhymes)

(1914)

Four brief songs for medium voice
and eight solo instruments

I. Kornílo (Kornílo)

II. Natáška (Little Natalie)

III. Polkóvnik (The Colonel)

IV. Stári͡et͡s i zái͡at͡s (The Old Man and the Hare)

•

Traditional Russian texts adapted by the composer

French singing version by Charles-Ferdinand Ramuz
German singing version by R. S. Hoffmann

Preface, Transliteration and English translation
by Stanley Appelbaum

INSTRUMENTATION

Voice [Canto, Cto.]

Flute [Flauto grande, Fl.]

Oboe [Oboe, Ob.]
doubles English Horn [Corno inglese, Cor. ingl.]

Clarinet in A, B♭ [Clarinetto, Cl. (La, Si♭)]

Bassoon [Fagotto, Fg.]

Solo strings:

Violin [Violino, Vl.]

Viola [Viola, Vla.]

Cello [Violoncello, Vlc.]

Bass [Contrabasso, Cb.]

TRANSLATOR'S PREFACE

Internationally acclaimed since 1910 for his Diaghilev ballet scores, Stravinsky resided in the French-speaking part of Switzerland during the First World War, prevented from returning to Russia, first by the hostilities, then by the Revolution. Reimmersing himself nostalgically in Russian folkways, he transformed traditional subjects into works that some critics regard as his best and most creative. In these war years, together with such larger works as *Renard, Histoire du Soldat,* and *Les Noces,* innovative in both music and stagecraft, he produced three short song cycles for one voice and a cycle for women's chorus, all set to old folk texts. A number of these works, both longer and shorter ones, deal with nursery rhymes and fables, for, after all, the composer was also bringing up four small children at the time.

The first composition completed during the war was *Pribaoutki* (Pribaútki; Nonsense Rhymes), four brief songs for solo voice and eight solo instruments. Written in the towns of Salvan and Clarens in August and September of 1914, they were first published (by Hann in Geneva and Chester in London) in 1917, with a dedication to the composer's (first) wife. They received their world-premiere performance at the Salle Gaveau, Paris, in May of 1919, and their first American performance at Aeolian Hall, New York, in December of the same year.

Published sketches of these songs indicate the consummate craftsmanship that underlay Stravinsky's genius. He set the words meticulously, first plotting out their metrical scansion when spoken aloud.

Short and witty, the *Pribaoutki* are far from trivial. To set these traditional texts, Stravinsky used a generally diatonic vocal line that was in a folk vein, but original with him. In many places he employed the technique, which was to become typical of his vocal works, of creating a tension between the normal word stress and the musical beat. The eight solo instruments illustrate and comment on the texts in musical lines that are more heterophonic than polyphonic; they add harmonic spice, leaving many discords unresolved.

The texts present numerous difficulties to those who were not brought up in the old folk culture. Some of the vocabulary is extremely rare, and the word forms can be archaic and dialectal. The texts are full of fanciful word plays suggested by the opportunity for clever rhymes and by other linguistic features. In the third song, for instance, every word but one begins with a *p*-sound—not to mention internal rhymes (such as *pod li͡od*) and the variations on a single verb stem by adding different prefixes (*pála propála . . . popála*). Since, in the case of these song texts, the sound is the "message," the translator has supplied a careful transliteration, including word stresses, for the benefit of those unused to the Cyrillic alphabet. (This transliteration is also helpful because Russian word breaks are often unclear in the text on the music pages.)

The German singing version on the music pages was written by R. S. Hoffmann; the French version, by the distinguished Swiss novelist Charles-Ferdinand Ramuz, who also worked with Stravinsky on the French versions of *Renard, Histoire du Soldat,* and *Les Noces.* It should be clearly understood that these two versions, the German and the French, were never intended to be strict translations of the Russian. They are, in their fashion, equivalents of it, starting out with the germinal idea of the Russian, but going their own way to create their own prosody and rhyme schemes, and their own brand of nonsense. (The German is somewhat closer to the Russian throughout than the French is.)

To give only a single example: Where the Russian translates literally as "The ducks started playing on their shawms, The cranes came out to dance, Thrusting out their long legs And stretching out their long necks," the German literally says "The little duck must play a shawm, the crane performs a round dance, stretching its neck in rage and fury, and strutting on one leg," while the French has "The ducks begin to blow into their cracked kazoos. There is the rooster, replying to them, and the hens turning in a circle."

The English translation provided here, facing the transliteration, is as literal as possible. Discussions of these texts by some non-Russian musicologists leave some doubts as to the completeness of their understanding; for instance, one author states that, in the third song, the priest caught the quail, just the opposite of what the Russian says. The same writer states that, in the first half of the second song, Natashka is being seduced. Not on the face of it, though it's possible if the loaf and the oven are taken as anatomical double-entendres!

In the first song, the violin twice has the direction "*jeté*" (flung). This, equivalent to the Italian *gettato,* or *spiccato,* indicates a vigorous bounce of the bow off the strings, each bounce taking in the notes included within the dashes or dots.

TEXT AND TRANSLATION

I. Kornílo

Nútko, di͡ádi͡uška Kornílo,
Zapri͡agáĭ-ko tï kobĭ́lu,
U Makár'i͡a na pi͡eskú
Prirazmĭ́č' gori͡e-toskú:
Stóit brážka v tui͡askú,
Brážka p'i͡ánai͡a p'i͡aná,
Vi͡esi͡elá k͡hmi͡el'nái͡a golová!
Brážku pórni͡aĭ vïpiváĭ!

I. Kornilo

Come now, dear Uncle Kornilo,
Harness the mare,
And at Makarii's place on the sand flat
Dispel your sorrows and cares:
There's beer in the little birchbark drinking vessel,
A really intoxicating beer,
And your head will spin merrily!
Drink up the beer heartily!

II. Natáška

Natáška, Natáška!
Sladi͡ónka kulážka,
Sladká mi͡odovái͡a,
V pi͡ečí ni͡e bïvála,
Žarú ni͡e vidála.
Zaigráli útki v dúdki,
Žiravlí pošlí pli͡asát',
Dólgi nógi vïstavli͡át',
Dólgi ši͡éi proti͡agát'.

II. Natáška (Little Natalie)

Nataška, Nataška!
The rye dough is nice and sweet,
Sweet with honey in it,
But it hasn't been in the oven,
It hasn't seen any heat.
The ducks started playing on their shawms,
The cranes came out to dance,
Thrusting out their long legs
And stretching out their long necks.

III. Polkóvnik

Pošól polkóvnik poguli͡át′,
Poĭmál ptíčku pi͡eri͡epi͡óločku;
Ptíčka pi͡eri͡epi͡óločka
Pit′ pok͡hoti͡éla,
Podni͡alás′ poleti͡éla,
Pála propála,
Pod li͡od popála,
Popá poĭmála,
Popá popóviča,
Pi͡etrá Pi͡etróviča.

III. The Colonel

A colonel went out for amusement,
He caught a little bird, a female quail;
The little bird, the female quail,
Got thirsty,
It rose up and flew away,
It fell, it got lost,
It got stuck under the ice,
It caught a priest,
A priest who was son of a priest
And whose name was Peter Petrovich.

IV. Stári͡et͡s i zái͡at͡s

Stóit grad pust,
A vo grádi͡e kust;
V kusti͡é sidít stári͡et͡s
Da várit izvári͡et͡s;
Pribi͡ežál kosóĭ zái͡at͡s
I prósit izvári͡et͡s.
I prikazál stári͡et͡s bi͡eznógomu bi͡ežát′,
A bi͡ezrúkomu k͡hvatát′,
A gólomu v pázuk͡hu klast′.

IV. The Old Man* and the Hare

There is a deserted city (OR: enclosure, garden),
And in the city is a bush;
In the bush sits an old man
Cooking onion gruel;
A squint-eyed hare ran up to him
And asked for some of the gruel.
And the old man ordered a legless man to run,
And an armless man to grasp things,
And a naked man to store things in his shirt front.

*The Russian word translated here generically as "old man" also has a specific meaning: a layman highly regarded among his neighbors as an authority on religious matters. Sometimes it is translated as "monk."

I.

Kornílo (Kornílo)

Cto.
-гай - ко ты ко - бы-(ы-ы)-лу, У Ма - ка - рья на пес - ку-(у-у-у)
trop de mauvais sang, laisse al-ler tout droit ta ju - ment
spann mit gutem Mu(u-u)-te, ein die al - te braune Stu(u-u)-te
Fl.
Ob.
Cl.
Fg.
gliss. come sopra
pizz.
arco gliss.
Vl.
arco sul Do-D
pizz.
Vla.
Vlc.
Cb.
5
ffp sub.
poco rit.
Poco meno mosso ♩ = 84
При-(и - и)-раз-мычь го - ре-тос - ку-(у-у): Сто - итъ бражка въ туяс-ку,
à l'au - ber-ge du Che-val Blanc: Là est un jo - li vin clair,
fah-(ah-ah)r im Nu dem Wirtshaus zu(u-u). Schäumt im Kru-ge hell das Bier,
come sopra
jété
10
sfp sub.

Cto.
Бражка пьяна - я пьяна, Ве - се - ла хмель-на - я го - ло - ва!
qui fait so - leil dans le verre; le jo - li vin rend le coeur con - tent:
al - le Sorgen schwinden dir, hel - len Kopf bringst du dir dann nachhaus.
Fl.
Ob.
Cl.
Fg.
Vl.
Vla.
Vlc.
Cb.
15
Бра - жку порняй вы - пи-вай!..
noie ton chag - rin de - dans.
Trin - - ke, On-kel, trink' nur aus!
Cadenza
mp
pp
lunga, colla parte
ff
pizz.
f
gliss.
sfff
20

II.
Natáška (Little Natalie)

(♩. = ♩) Meno mosso ♩ = 100
Cto.
За иг-гра-ли ут - ки въ дуд-ки, Жи-ра-вли по-шли пля-сать,
Les ca-nards com-mencent à — souffler dans leurs mir - li - tons cre - vés.
Ent-lein muß Schal-mei - en — bla-sen, Kra-nich tanzt den Rin-gel-reihn,
Fl.
Cor. ingl.
Cl.
Fg.
mp
sempre simile
pizz.
sim.
Vl.
arco, sul Do-D (sempre)
Vla.
Vlc.
Cb.
arco
sfp
Дол - ги но - ги вы-став-лять, Дол-ги ше - и про - тя - гать,
Voi - - là l'coq qui leur ré - pond et les poul's qui tournent en rond.
streckt den Hals in Wut und Ra - sen und stelzt auf ei - nem Bein.
mf
sf
arco
pizz.
sff
15

III.
Polkóvnik (The Colonel)

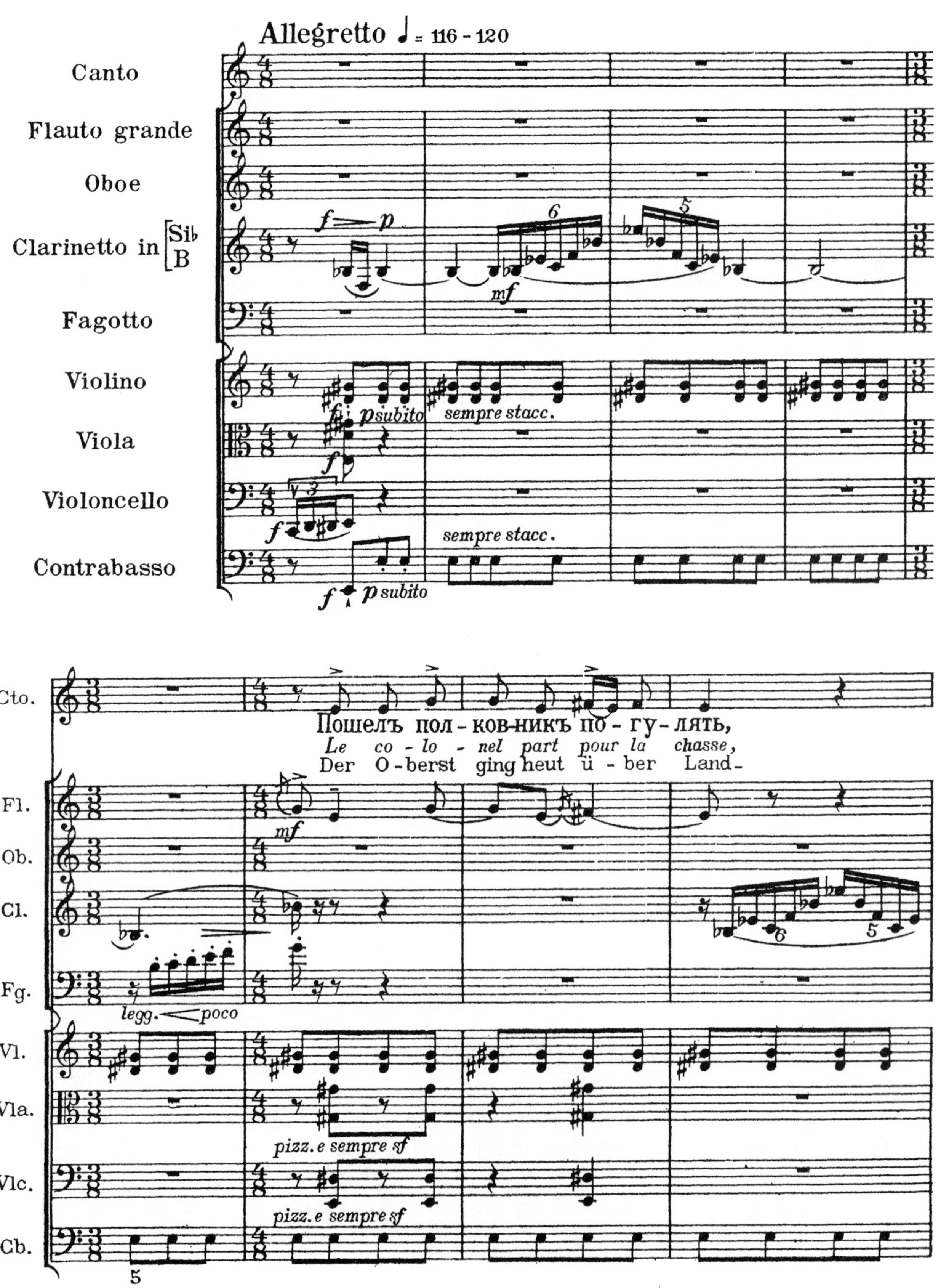

Cto.
Fl.
Ob.
Cl.
Fg.
Vl.
Vla.
Vlc.
Cb.
mp
10
sf
mf
Поймалъ птичку пе - ре - пё-лоч - ку;
tir' sur un' bé - cass',manqu' sa bé - casse,
fing sich ei - ne Wach-tel mit der Hand_
15

Cto.
Fl.
Ob.
Cl.
Fg.
Vl.
Vla.
Vlc.
Cb.
mp
mf
f
5
20
Пти - чка пе-ре - пё-ло - чка Пить по-хо-тѣ-ла, По - днялась
tir' sur un' per - drix, — la per- drix s'en-fuit, — tombé et cass'
Was - ser woll-te sie krie-gen, drum mit Ver-gnü gen tat sie von
cresc.
25

Cto.
Fl.
Ob.
Cl.
Fg.
Vl.
Vla.
Vlc.
Cb.
по-ле-тѣ-ла, Па-ла про-па-ла, Подъ лёдъ по-па-ла, По
son fu-sil; il ap-pell' son chien, son chien n'ré-pond rien; sa
dan-nen flie-gen. Plumps lag sie un-ten, im Was-ser drun-ten hat
pizz. sempre
cresc.
arco
pizz.
30
Doppio movimento ♩ = 60
rit.
па пой-ма-ла, По-па по-по-ви-ча, Пе-тра-Пе-тро-ви-ча.
femm' l'a re-çu, sa femm' l'a bat-tu... Chass'-ra jamais plus.
sie ge-fun-den der Po-pe Po-po-witsch, der Pe-ter Pe-trowitsch.
dim.
pizz. e sf
arco sul La-A
poco sf

IV.

Stáriets i záiats (The Old Man and the Hare)

Cto
Въ кус - тѣ си-дитъ старецъ Да варитъ из-ва-рецъ; При-бѣ-
Et puis voi - là qu'le vieux, fait cuir' sa soup'sans feu Un
ein Greis sitzt seit Wo-chen, will sich Sup-pe ko-chen. Kommt ein
Fl.
Cor. ingl.
Cl.
Fg.
Vl.
Vla.
Vlc.
Cb.
pizz.
arco sul pont.
15
Cto
жалъ ко-сой за-яцъ И про - ситъ из-ва-рецъ.
liè - vre sur la route, lui de - - man - de sa soupe.
Ha - se her-für: „Gib die Sup - pe mir."
Fl.
Cor. ingl.
Cl.
Fg.
Vl.
Vla.
Vlc.
Cb.
20

Con moto ♩ = 66
Cto.
Fl.
Cor. ingl.
Cl.
Fg.
Vl.
Vla.
Vlc.
Cb.
sfp
mf
sf
p
pizz.
arco
И при - ка - залъ ста-рецъ без - но - го - му бѣ - жать,
Et l'vieux a dit comm' ça, au bos-su d'se te - nir droit,
Der Greis dann ge-sagt hat: Oh-ne Arm wer ge - packt hat,

Cto.
Fl.
Cor. ingl.
Cl.
Fg.
Vl.
Vla.
Vlc.
Cb.
А __ без-ру-ко-
au manchot d'é-
oh-ne Bein wer noch
му хва тать, __
tendr' les bras __
sprin-gen kann __
А го-ло-му въ па-
et au mu-et d'par-
und oh-ne Keh-le
40
45

Tempo I ♪= 166
Cto.
зу-ху класть.
ler plus bas.
sin-gen kann.
Fl.
Cor. ingl.
Cl.
Fg.
mp
f
mf
arco, sul pont.
fp
sf
Vl.
Vla.
Vlc.
Cb.
50
55
pizz.
p

Very respectfully dedicated
to Madame the Princess Edmond de Polignac

Renard
(The Fox)

A burlesque in song and dance in one act
for clowns, dancers, and acrobats,
with large chamber ensemble and four men's voices

(1915–16)

•

Russian text by the composer,
adapted from the folktale collection by Afanasiev

French singing version by Charles-Ferdinand Ramuz
German singing version by Rupert Koller

Note and synopsis by Stanley Appelbaum

INSTRUMENTATION

°[Piccolo [Fl. picc.]
Flute [Flauto grande, Fl. gr.]

°[Oboe [Ob.]
English Horn [Corno inglese, Cor. ingl.]

°[Clarinet in E♭ [Clarinetto piccolo, Cl. picc. (Mi♭)]
Clarinet in A, B♭ [Cl. (La, Si♭)]

Bassoon [Fagotto, Fg.]

2 Horns in F [Corni, Cor. (Fa)]
Trumpet in A, B♭ [Tromba, Tr. (La, Si♭)]

Cimbalom°° [Cimb. hungar., Cimb.]

Timpani (Pedal) [Timp., Timb(ale) à levier]

Percussion:
Tambourine with jingles [T.d.B. (Tambour de Basque) à grelots]
Tambourine without jingles [T.d.B. sans grelots]
Small Side Drum [Caisse claire, C. cl., C. c. P.]
Triangle [Triangolo, Trgl.]
Cymbals [Piatti(e), Ptti.]
Bass Drum [Gran cassa, Gr. c.]

(For a list of percussion beaters, see the Glossary, p. v, under *baguette*.)

Singers:
2 Solo Tenors [Tenori I, II]
2 Solo Basses [Bassi I, II]

Solo Strings:
Violin I [Violino I, Vl.]
Violin II [Violino II, Vl.]
Viola [Viola, Vla.]
Cello [Violoncello, Vlc.]
Bass [Contrabasso, Cb.]

°one player

°°The cimbalom, a type of dulcimer traditionally found in the Magyar orchestra, is played by striking its array of open strings with small beaters. The sound varies according to the kind of "stick" (*baguette*)—either leather-tipped (*en cuir*) or wooden-tipped (*en bois*)—and its placement on the string: in the center or near the bridge (*près du chevalet*). Some modern instruments have a damper pedal, permitting an increasingly resonant sound (*ouvrez peu à peu la Pédale*), or a resounding sound (*cuivrez*). Although the cimbalom's complete chromatic compass extends from E below the bass staff to the E four octaves higher, Stravinsky's score provides alternate passages for an instrument with a low D (*pour l'instrument qui possède le ré grave*).

NOTES

The chamber opera *Renard* was commissioned by the Princess Edmond de Polignac, whose Parisian salon Stravinsky had attended, and the work is dedicated to her. It is one of the intensely Russian pieces written during the composer's wartime sojourn in the French-speaking area of Switzerland, 1914–1920. It was composed in the years 1915 and 1916, but not performed until 1922, when it was produced by Diaghilev in Paris to designs by Mikhail Larionov. The composer later told interviewers that he had made no conscious use of authentic folk melodies.

Stravinsky intended the characters' roles to be performed in mime by clowns, dancers and acrobats, all of whom remain constantly on stage between the entrance and exit marches. The vocalists, two tenors and two basses, were meant to sit in the small orchestra, which included a Hungarian cimbalom that Stravinsky had discovered and purchased in a Geneva café. The orchestra was to sit behind the dancers, sharing their podium, unless the performance was in a theater, in which case the dancing was to be done in front of the curtain. (In Larionov's design, the characters wore animal masks that sat atop their heads and did not cover the full face; the Rooster's tree was a simple platform on a post with a ladder reaching to the stage floor.) The four voices are generally not linked to specific characters, although in the dialogues between the Rooster and the Fox, the Rooster's lines are frequently assigned to Tenor I, the fox's to Tenor II.

The Russian text (the original one) was written by Stravinsky himself, who adapted folktales from the famous collection by Afanasiev, the Russian "Grimm." The verbal and conceptual world is that of the old peasantry and the language is quite specialized, including folklike diminutives, colloquial word forms, regional vocabulary and liturgical Old Church Slavonic forms (in the Fox's role as a nun). Furthermore, words are distorted for comic effect, and are often there more for their sound than for their sense: for instance, the opening fivefold *Kudá?* ("Where to?"—presumably with the connotation "Where has he gotten to?") resembles a rooster's call. The Russian title is *Báĭka*, meaning "a narrative."

The French version, by the composer's new Swiss friend Charles-Ferdinand Ramuz, a distinguished regional novelist who also worked with Stravinsky on *Histoire du soldat* and other projects, was based on a word-for-word French translation provided by the composer, but the final result is not, and never was, intended as a literal or even close translation. Instead, it is an independent singing version, less concerned with preserving the meaning than with fitting the music exactly and with (largely) respecting the original rhyme scheme and even the original vowel coloring: note that the first words of the French, the fivefold "Où ça?" ("Where?") have the same vowel sounds as *Kudá?* As far as the meaning is concerned, the French occasionally translates the Russian, but much more often is an extremely free adaptation that is equally suitable to the action that is taking place. (The German text in the present volume, by Rupert Koller, often hews closely to the French, but also goes its own way much of the time.)

For many of the above considerations, and because words are frequently repeated, either exactly or with slight variations, it is not feasible to offer a complete exact translation of the original Russian text in libretto form. What follows, instead, is a tight, detailed synopsis of the Russian, with references to the pages of the score.

Renard: A Synopsis

The dancers enter to a march (pp. 25–27). The Rooster calls for the capture of a hated person whom he wants to trample, split with an axe, stab and hang (pp. 28–41). "I sit in the oak tree," he continues, "I guard the house and I sing a song" (pp. 42–43). The Fox (a female character) arrives disguised as a nun and urges the Rooster to come down and make confession, saying she has come, hungry and thirsty, from a distant wilderness for that purpose (pp. 43–46). The Rooster recognizes the Fox and says sarcastically that he hasn't fasted or prayed, so: "Come another time" (p. 47). The Fox/Nun accuses the Rooster of having evil thoughts and too many wives; some men have ten, twenty or forty and, whenever they meet, fight over their wives as if over concubines; the Rooster should come down and not die in sin (pp. 48–55). The Rooster leaps to the ground and is seized by the Fox, who drags him around the stage; the Rooster laments that he is being carried off over rugged terrain to the ends of the earth (pp. 55–58).

The Rooster calls on the Cat and the Ram for aid (pp. 59–62). They appear and ask the Fox if she isn't going to share her easily gained catch, since they are hungry and aggressive (pp. 63–67). The Fox releases the Rooster and runs off; the Rooster, Cat and Ram dance (p. 68). They mock the Fox's boastfulness, and sing of how the Rooster left the barnyard with his hens and was greeted by the Fox, who expected a meal, how the Rooster begged not to be eaten and offered the hens instead; the Fox wanted the Rooster only, grabbed him and carried him far off, the Rooster shrieked for help but the hens didn't hear (pp. 69–88). The Cat and the Ram depart and the Rooster regains his perch (pp. 88–89).

The Fox returns, casts off her nun's robe and, complimenting the Rooster on his appearance, asks him to look out the window and receive peas as a reward; the Rooster refuses, saying he prefers cereal; the Fox then says she has a big house full of wheat; the Rooster says he's full; the Fox offers a pancake, the Rooster isn't fooled; again the Fox asks the Rooster to descend so she can carry his soul up to heaven (pp. 89–105). The Rooster prepares to jump down, and the First Tenor shouts, "Fox, don't eat meat on a fast day"; the Rooster jumps, the Fox seizes him, and the Second Tenor says: "It may be forbidden to some, but it's all right for us!" (p. 105). The Rooster makes the same lament as before, and appeals to the Cat and Ram as before (pp. 106–112). The Fox carries the Rooster off to one side and starts to pluck him; the Rooster says that the Fox is expected for dinner at the home of the Rooster's father, where buttered *blinis, pirogi* and porridge await her; he then asks the Lord to remember and preserve all his relatives, naming them individually (pp. 113–122).

Just as the Rooster is passing out, the Cat and Ram appear and, to the accompaniment of a *gusli* (psaltery), they sing a soothing song: "Is Ivanova the Fox at home in her golden lair with her little children?"; they name the Fox's daughters (pp. 122–134). The Fox sticks the tip of her nose out of her earth and asks who is calling her; they say that animals are coming with a scythe [they themselves have one!] to cut her up, that they have watched so that the animals didn't eat her up, and that they have run to prevent the animals from tearing her apart, etc.; then they catch her by the tail, drag her out by it and throttle her (pp. 135–149). The Rooster, Cat and Ram dance and sing in mockery of the Fox's unexpected death; most of the song text is an untranslatable farrago of folk sayings barely related to the plot (pp. 150–170). The dancers exit to a reprise of the opening march (pp. 171–172).

STANLEY APPELBAUM

MARCHE [MARCH]

Entrance of the Actors

III
Fg.
Cor. (Fa)
2.
Tr. (La)
Pttl.e Gr.C.
15
fff
ff
étouf-fez
20
Fine
IIII
Fl.picc.
ff marcatissimo
Ob.
ff
simile
Cl.picc. (Mib)
ff marcatissimo
1.
f marcato
Cimb. hungar.
forte
T.d.B. a grelots
avec le pouce
coup de genoux
25

IV
Fl.picc.
Ob.
Cl.picc. (Mib)
1.
Cor. (Fa)
Cimb.
T.d.B.
30
V
Fl.picc.= Fl.gr.
Oboe= Cor.ingl.
Fg.
come sopra
Cor. (Fa)
Tr. (La)
forte
Cimb.
étouffez subito
Trgl. T.d.B.
Ptti.e Gr.C.
35
Da capo al Fine

*) Les notes marqués du signe „o" se jouent derrière le chevalet de l'instrument

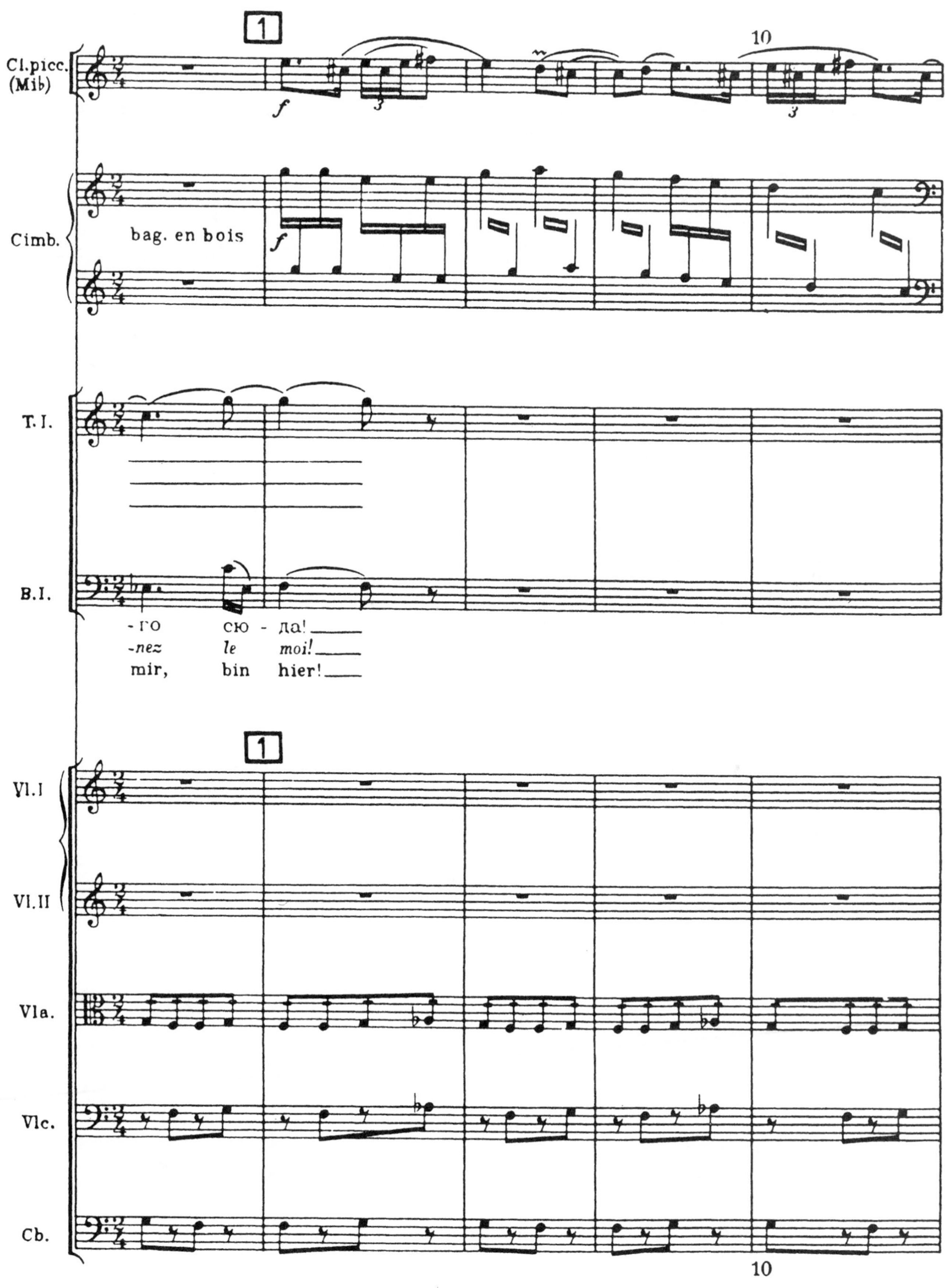
1
10
Cl.picc. (Mib)
Cimb.
bag. en bois
T. I.
B. I.
-го сю - да!
-nez le moi!
mir, bin hier!
1
Vl. I
Vl. II
Vla.
Vlc.
Cb.
10

2
15
Fl.gr.
Cor. ingl.
Cl.picc. (Mib)
Fg.
Cor. (Fa)
mf stacc.
Tr. (Sib)
mf stacc.
Cimb.
bag. en cuir
T. I
Я — но - га-ми стопчу,
Et on lui cass'ra les os,
Will ihm die Knochen bre-chen.
T. II
То - по-
On lui
Will ihn
2
Vla.
Vlc.
Cb.
15

Fl.gr.
Cor. ingl.
Cl.picc. (Mib)
Fg.
Cor. (Fa)
1. Solo-forte
Cimb.
Timp.
T. I
T. II
-ромъ срублю.
plant'-ra l'cou-teau
ab - ste-chen
B. II
Я-(а) но -
Et on vous lui
Wol-len ihm die
Vl. I
pizz.
Vl. II
(arco)
Vla.
Vlc.
Cb.
20
3

25
Cimb.
T.I
Ку-да, ку - да, ку-да, ку-
Où ça, où ça, où ça où
Oh Gott, oh Gott, oh Gott, was
B.II
-га ми стопчу, И то-(о) по - ромъ срублю.
cass'-ra les os, on vous lui plan - t'ra le cou-teau
Kno-chen bre-chen, wol-len ihn ab - ste-chen.
Vl.I
Vl.II
Vla.
Vlc.
Cb.
25

4
30
Cor. ingl.
Cor. (Fa)
Cimb.
T. I
-да, ку - да?
ça, où ça?
wird aus mir?
B. I
По - дай-те мнѣ е - го сю - да!
Où est il? a - me-nez le moi!
Bringt ihn doch schon her bin hier.
B. II
По - дай - те мнѣ е - го ско рѣй сю.-
Et puis plus vit' que ça! Voi - là... voi -
Was braucht ihr lang', nur schnell da - her zu
4
(pizz.)
Vl. I
pizz.
Vl. II
Vla.
Vlc.
Cb.
30

35
Cimb.
bag. en bois
Фальцетъ
fausset
Falsett
B.I
Ку-да, ку - да, ку-да, ку - да, ку-да, ку - да?
O ça, où ça, où ça, où ça, où ça, où ça?
Oh Gott, oh Gott, oh Gott, oh Gott, was wird aus mir?
B.II
-да!
là!
mir.
Ку -
Où
Bin
Vl.I
Vl.II
Vla.
Vlc.
Cb.
35

5
Fl.gr.
Cl.picc. (Mi♭)
Cimb.
T.II
И ____ но - жи - шко здѣ - ся,
Et le p'tit cou - teau, on l'a
Hab'n ein schar - fes Mes - ser - lein.
B.I
И ____ но - жи - шко здѣ - ся,
Et le p'tit cou - teau, on l'a
Hab'n ein schar - fes Mes - ser - lein.
B.II
да!
ça?
hier!
5
stacc.
arco
Vl.I
subito f
stacc.
arco
Vl.II
subito f
Vla.
Vlc.
Cb.

6
40
Fl.gr.
Cl.picc. (Mib)
Fg.
Cor. (Fa)
Tr. (Sib)
Cimb.
T.I
T.II
B.I
B.II
И но-жи-шко здѣ ся, И гу-
le p'tit cou-teau, on l'a, et la
Ja, ein Mes-ser-lein und ein
6
Vl.I
Vl.II
Vla.
Vlc.
Cb.
f
mf
ff
40

45
Fl.gr.
Cl.picc. (Mi♭)
Fg.
Cor. (Fa)
Tr. (Si♭)
Cimb.
T.I
-жи - шко здѣ - ся,
corde aus - si, on l'a,
Schnür-chen gar fein,
T.II
-жи - шко здѣ - ся,
corde aus - si, on l'a,
Schnür-chen gar fein,
B.I
-жи - шко здѣ - ся,
corde aus - si, on l'a,
Schnür-chen gar fein,
B.II
-жи - шко здѣ - ся,
corde aus - si, on l'a,
Schnür-chen gar fein,
Vl.I
Vl.II
sul sol
Vla.
Vlc.
Cb.
45

7
50
Fl.gr.
Cor. ingl.
Cl.picc. (Mi♭)
Fg.
Cor. (Fa)
stacc.
Tr. (Si♭)
Cimb.
bag. en cuir
T. I
T. II
B. I
B. II
И за-рѣжемъ здѣ - ся, И по - вѣ-симъ здѣ - - ся.
et i - ci on l'crev' - ra, et i - ci on l'pen - - dra.
ab - zu - ste - chen, auf - zu - hän - gen Gok - ke - lein.
7
Vl. I
Vl. II
Vla.
Vlc.
Cb.
50

8
Fl.gr. = Fl.picc.
55
Fl.gr.
Cl.picc. (Mi♭)
Cl.picc. in Mi♭ = Cl. in Si♭
Fg.
Cor. (Fa)
Tr. (Si♭)
Cimb.
Timp.
Gr.C.
T.I
Куда, куда, куда, куда, куда, куда?
Où ça, où ça, où ça, où ça, où ça?
Oh Gott, oh Gott, oh Gott, was soll das sein?
B.II
И но... и но - жишко здѣ-ся,
et le p'tit cou - cou-teau, on l'a,
Hier das schar-fe Mes-ser-lein und
8
Vl.I
Vl.II
Vla.
Vlc.
Cb.
pizz.
sff
sf
f
55

60
Cimb.
Timp.
Gr.C.
B.II
И гу... и гу - жи - шко здѣ ся, И за... и за - рѣжемъ здѣ - ся,
la p'tit' co - corde aus - si on l'a et i - ci on vous l'crè - crè - v'ra
da ein Schnür-chen, stark und fein, um ab - zu - ste - chen, auf - zu - hän - gen,
Vl.I
Vl.II
Vla.
Vlc.
Cb.
60

Meno mosso (♩ = 63)
9
Cor. ingl.
fff
Fg.
Cimb.
Ped.
Timp.
Gr.C.
B. II
И по...и по - вѣсимъздѣся.
et i - ci on vous l'pen-pen-dra.
ab - zu - ste-chen, auf - zu-hän-gen.
9
Meno mosso (♩ = 63)
Vl. I
Vl. II
Vla.
Vlc.
Cb.

65
10
Cor. ingl.
Fg.
Cor. (Fa)
Tr. (Sib)
T. I
con sord.
Сижу на
Je suis sur
Von meiner
10
pizz.
Vla.
poco sf
sul do
arco
Vlc.
pizz.
sempre simile
pizz.
Cb.
65
poco sf (sempre)

Cor. ingl.
Fg.
Cor. (Fa)
Tr. (Sib)
T. I
ду - бу, Си жу, домъ сте-ре-гу, Пѣсню по-ю.
mon bâ-ton, je garde la mai-son, j'chant'ma chanson.
War-te aus, sing ich in al - le Welt hinaus ich wahr' dies Haus.
(arco)
(pizz.)
Vlc.
Cb.
70
Cor. ingl. = Oboe
Cor. ingl.
Fg.
Cor. (Fa)
Cimb.
Ped.
Timp.
(Приходитъ лиса въ одѣянiи монахини.)
(Arrive Renard en costume de religieuse)
pizz.
Vlc.
75
(Der Fuchs kommt als Mönch verkleidet)

11
Cl. (Sib)
Fg.
T. II
Здравствуй, кра-сно-е ча-до, пѣ-телъ! Сни-ди,
Sa - lut, mon cher fils à la toque roug'! Des-cen-
Gott mit dir, du treff-li-cher Sän-ger, teu-res
sul Sol
arco
Vl. I
sul Ré
Cb.
80
Ob.
Cl. (Sib)
Fg.
T. II
кра-сно-е ча-до, на зем-лю, Да по-кай-ся!
dez, cher fils, du lieu de votr' sé-jour, et con-fes-sez-vous.
Söhnchen, steig' nie-der vom Thro-ne, beicht' dei-ne Sün-den!
Vl. I
(pizz.)
Vla.
(pizz.)
Vlc.
Cb.

12
85
Ob.
Cl. (Sib)
Fg.
Cor. (Fa)
Cimb.
sim.
senza Ped.
(Пѣтухъ въ сердцахъ)
(Le coq, impatienté)
(Der Hahn voll Unruhe)
rall. accel. a tempo rall. accel. a tempo
T. I
Поди вонъ лиса!
Zut! mèr' Re-nard!
Schau, daß d'weiterkommst.
T. II
Я шла изъ дальнихъ пу-стынь, Не пи-ла, не ѣ-ла...
J'viens du fond des dé-serts, n'ai ni bu, ni man-gé...
Weit — aus ö - den Wüste-nei'n komm ich her, bei dir zu sein.
Vla.
Vlc.
arco
Cb.
pizz.

Ob.
Cl. (Si♭)
Fg.
con sord.
Tr. (Si♭)
non cuivré
(Лиса продолжаетъ)
(Renard continuant)
(Der Fuchs fährt fort)
T. II
Мно-го ну-жды пре - тер пѣ-(ѣ) ла; Те - бя, ми-ло - е ча -
Ai, souf-fert beaucoup d'mi-sers; j'suis i-ci, fils très cher,
Ohn' Speis' und Trank, von We-ges Müh'n krank, komm ich die See-le dein, be -
Vl. I
Vl. II
(pizz.)
arco
Vla.
Ob.
Cl. (Si♭)
Fg.
f sub.
Tr. (Si♭)
T. II
- до! Спо - вѣ - - дать хо - тѣ - (ѣ) - ла.
a fin d'vous con - fes - ser*)
wah - ren vor ew'-ger Not und Pein.
Vl. I
Vl. II
Vla.
90

*) Prononcez: confessère

13 Più mosso (Tempo I) ♩= 126
Ob.
Cimb.
(Пѣтухъ съ задоромъ)
(Le coq avec arrogance)
(Der Hahn witzig)
T. II
О, ма-(а)-ти мо-я, ли-си- -ца! Я не по-стил-
O ma-(a) bonn' viell' mèr' Re-nard, ces mo-o-o-
Ach, ehr-würd'ger Va-ter, mir, ist's sehr leid, g'rad so un-ge-
13 Più mosso (Tempo I) ♩= 126
Vlc.
sempre f e molto stacc.
arco
Cb.
sempre f e molto stacc.
Fl. picc.
Ob.
Fg.
Cimb.
T. I
-ся, не мо-ли-лся; Придивъин-но-е вре- -мя.
m'ries lù j'n'g crois pas; re-pass' voir une aut' fois.
-le-gen ihr kom-men seid. Hab' heut' lei-der wirk-lich nicht Zeit.
Vlc.
Cb.
95

14 Meno mosso ♩ = 63
Cl. (Sib)
Fg.
Cor. (Fa)
rall. accel. a tempo rall. accel.
T. II
О — мо - е ча — до, пѣтелъ! Си - (и)дишь ты на ви - -
O — mon fils très cher, vous êt's as - sis très haut —
Oh, — mein lie - ber Sohn! All - zu - hoch sitz'st du —
Vla.
Vlc.
pizz. arco saltando (arco) gliss.
100
15
Cl. (Sib)
Fg.
a tempo
T. II
- со - цемъ дре - вѣ, Да мы - слишь мы - сли не - до - бры - я,
dans les airs, mais ça n'em pêch' pas que tu èrr's, prends
auf dei - nem Thro - ne! Und wahr - lich voll bist du bö - ser Ge - dan - ken,
Vl. I
Vla.
Vlc.
sul Sol
105

16
colla parte
Fl.picc.= Fl.gr.
Fl.picc.
Cor. (Fa)
mf
Tr. (Sib)
(sord.)
p
senza sord.
Cimb.
sf
senza Ped.
rall.
accel.
a tempo
T. II
про - кля-ты - я
gard' mon fils.
gott - lo - sen Sinn's!
Вы де - ржи - те женъ по мно - гу;—
Vous a - vez, vous autr's beau - coup trop de femm's;
Sieh, ihr al - le ha-bet viel zu viel Frau'n:
16
colla parte
Vl. I
Vl. II
pizz.
f
Vla.
Vlc.

17
115
Ob.
Fg.
Cor. (Fa)
Tr. (Sib)
Cimb.
T. II
(о) вре-(е)-ме-немъ до со-ро-ка! Гдѣ
a - vec le temps jus - qu'a qua-rant! Par - tout
— gar bis an die vier-zig, ja an vier-zig gehn! Wo ihr
Vl. I
Vl. II
Vla.
pizz.
pizz.
115

Ob.
Fg.
Cor. (Fa)
T. II
cresc.
cresc.
cresc.
сой - дё - тесь, тутъ и де-рё-тесь О сво-ихъ же-нахъ,
où vous vous ren-con - trez, vous vous bat-tez, rap - port à vos fem mes,
auch_ bei-sam-men seid, habt ihr um eu-re Eh-frau'n Streit, wie um
18 colla parte
p
poco
mf
rall.
accel.
какъ о на - ло - (о) - (о)-жницахъ. Сни - ди, ми - ло - е
comm' si c'é - taient vos maî - tress's; viens mon fils, jusqu'à
käuf - li - che Frau'ns-per - so - nen. Denk auch, mein lie - ber Sohn,
18 colla parte
Vl. I
Vl. II
Vla.
Vlc.
pizz.
(pizz.)
f gliss.
sul Do pizz.
120

a tempo
colla parte
125
Fg.
poco
Cor. (Fa)
poco
poco
con sord.
Tr. (Sib)
Timp.
gliss. pour la Timb. à levier
rall.
accel.
T. I
и по каи-ся, Да не во-грѣ-
a - - fin d'n'pas mou- -
Denk', du könn-test ster-ben müs-sen, ster - ben
T. II
ча - до, на зе-млю
moi et con - fess' toi,
an dein En - de.
и по каи-ся, Да не во-грѣ-
a - - fin d'n'pas mou- -
Denk', du könn-test ster-ben müs-sen, ster - ben
a tempo
colla parte
Vl. I
come sopra
Vl. II
come sopra
arco
pizz.
Vla.
come sopra
arco
pizz.
(pizz.)
Vlc.
come sopra
pizz. gliss.
Cb.
125

a tempo
19
colla parte
Fg.
Tr. (Sib)
gliss.
Timp.
Gr. C. Ptti.
etouffez subito
sff
lunga ad lib.
tr
Caisse claire
f
(Пѣтухъ готовитъ „salto mortale")
(Le coq se prépare à sauter „salto mortale")
(Der Hahn bereitet sich zum „Salto mortale")
(Спрыгнулъ)
(Il saute)
(er springt.)
T. I
p
-хахъ ум - рѣ - ши.
rir en é tat d'pé-ché.
in dei-nen Sün - den.
T. II
p
-хахъ ум - рѣ - ши.
rir en é tat d'pé-ché.
in dei-nen Sün - den.
a tempo
19
colla parte
Vla.
arco
Vlc.
arco
pizz.
Cb.
come sopra

20 Stringendo (♩.= 126)
130
Fl. gr.
Fg.
Cimb.
Timp.
sempre poco sf
(Лиса схвативаетъ пѣтуха и носится съ нимъ по сценѣ, держа его подмышкой)
(Renard saisit le coq et tourne autour de la scène en le tenant sous le bras)
(Der Fuchs stürzt sich auf den Hahn, ergreift ihn unter den Achseln und schleppt ihn über die Szene)
(Пѣтухъ отчаянно отбивается)
(Le coq se débattant désespérément)
(Der Hahn wehrt sich verzweifelt)
T. I
По - не - сла ме - ня ли - са, По - не - сла пѣ - ту -
Ah! mon Dieu! mon Dieu! mon Dieu! Il me tir' par la
Oh, mein Gott, o du mein Gott, hilf doch, er macht mich
20 Stringendo (♩.= 126)
(pizz.)
Vl. I
Vl. II
Vla.
stacc. e sempre sff
Vlc.
arco, stacc. e sff sempre
Cb.
arco, stacc. e sff sempre
130

Fl. gr.
come sopra
Fg.
Cimb.
Timp.
T. I
- ха, По - кру - тымъ бе-реж - - камъ, По вы - со - кимъ го -
queue... Il me tir' par la queue, il dé - chir' mes ha -
tot, er zerrt mich, zer-beißt mich, er zer - fetzt und zer -
Vl. I
Vl. II
Vla.
Vlc.
Cb.
21
Fl. gr.
Fg.
Tr. (Si♭)
(sord.)
sf
Cimb.
Timp.
T. I
- рамъ, Въчу - жі - я зе - мли, Въ да - ле - кі - я стра - ны,
bits, il me lâch' - ra plus Qu'à trent' six lieues d'i - ci,
reißt mich, mein schö - nes Kleid, mein schö - nes Fe - der - kleid,
Vl. II

Fl.gr.
Cl. (Si♭)
Fg.
Cor. (Fa)
non f e non cresc.
Tr. (Si♭)
sf
Cimb.
Timp.
T. I
За три девять земель, Въ тридцатое царство, Въ тридесятое государство;
(trois et trois qui font six, et trois fois trois qui font dix, et trois fois dix et six trent six!)
und verschleppt mich so weit, so weit — von hier, hat denn keiner Mitleid, Mitleid mit mir?
arco
Vl. I
sul Do
Vla.
135

*) Pour l'instrument qui a le ré grave exécuter:
Das Instrument, welches das tiefe d hat, spielt:

Fl. gr.
Ob.
Cl. (Sib)
Fg.
Cor. (Fa)
Tr. (Sib)
Cimb.
Timp.
C.cl.
T. I
Котъ да ба ранъ, Хо четъсъѣсть пѣ ту - ха!
frèr' bouc, frèr' chat, bons a mis, e - cou - tez moi,
Barm - her - zig - keit! E - wig will ich euch dank-bar sein
arco
pizz.
Vl. I
Vl. II
Vla.
Vlc.
Cb.
trem.

*) come sopra

23
o·= d. (d = 84)
Fl. gr.
Ob.
Cl. (Sib)
Fg.
Cor. (Fa)
marc.
Tr. (Sib)
Cimb.
*)
Timp.
Gr. C.
mf
C. cl.
T. I
Котъ да баранъ, О ты - ми - те ме -
frèr' bouc, frèr' chat, v'nez vit', ti - rez moi
in E - wig - keit. Werd' ich durch euch be -
T. II
f
О ты - ми - те ме -
v'nez vit', ti - rez moi
Werd' ich durch euch be -
23
o·= d. (d = 84)
Vl. I
arco
pizz.
Vl. II
arco
pizz.
Vla.
arco
pizz.
arco
Vlc.
Cb.

*) come sopra

♩. = 84
♩. = ♩ = 84
145
Fg.
sempre f e senza diminuendo
Cor. (Fa)
Cimb.
T. I
ня!
d'là!
freit.
T. II
ня!
d'là!
freit.
Vl. I
Vl. II
Vla.
Vlc.
Cb.
145

24 Con brio
𝅗𝅥 (42) = 𝅗𝅥. (= 42) = ♩ = 126
Fl. gr.
Ob.
Cl. (Si♭)
Fg.
Cor. (Fa)
Tr. (Si♭)
Cimb.
sub. f
Ped.
(Появляются, котъ да баранъ)
(Apparaissent le chat et le bouc)
(Kater und Bock treten auf)
24 Con brio
𝅗𝅥 (42) = 𝅗𝅥. (= 42) = ♩ = 126
arco
Vl. I
Vl. II
Vla.
Vlc.
Cb.

150
Fl. gr.
Ob.
Cl. (Sib)
Cl. in Sib = Cl. picc. in Mib
Fg.
Cor. (Fa)
Tr. (Sib)
Cimb.
(♮)
Vl. I
Vl. II
arco
Vla.
Vlc.
Cb.
150

Fl.gr. = Fl.picc.
Fl.
stacc.
Fg.
f
con sord.
Tr.
(Si♭)
Cimb.
B. I.
Эхъ ты, ку - му - шка - го - лу - - - бу-шка!
Eh! - - - ma bonn' viell' mèr' Re - nard,
Ei, da seht doch mal, der schlau-e Ge - vat-ter
Vl. I
Vl. II
Vla.
Vlc.
sf sempre
Cb.

25
Ob
Cl. picc. (Mi♭)
Fg.
Cor. (Fa)
Tr. (Si♭)
Cimb.
B. I
Не куп - лен-но-е у — те бя, де - ше - - во - е;
c'que tu as dans l'bec ne t'a pas coû - té cher,
hat sich bil - lig was recht Gu - tes er - gat - tert;
25
Vl. I
Vl. II
Vla.
Vlc.
Cb.
f marcato

Cor.
(Fa)
Cimb.
Timp.
B. I
Ужъ не— по-дѣлишь-ли мясца? Аль не вѣ-даешь Ер - макъ
ne vou - drais tu pas t'en dé-fair'? on ___ est des bons chré - tiens,
Willst al - lein 'nen Sonn-tags - bra-ten, gib ihn her, laß dir gut ra-ten,
B. II
155
Ужъ не по-дѣлишь-ли мясца? Аль не вѣ-даешь Ер - макъ
ne vou - drais tu pas t'en dé-fair'? on ___ est des bons chré - tiens,
Willst al - lein 'nen Sonn-tags - bra-ten, gib ihn her, laß dir gut ra-ten,
Cimb.
Timp.
T. I
И те - бѣ ___ то - го не ми - но - вать!
Al-lons! donn' - nous ça, ou bien on t'fout bas!
Doch hör' recht wohl — gib ihn wil - lig, sonst!
B. I
За - тре - щалъ на - тощакъ.
on te pai - (e) - ra bien.
woll'n ihn nicht— umsonst.
B. II
За - тре - щалъ на - тощакъ.
on te pai - (e) - ra bien.
woll'n ihn nicht umsonst.
Vl. I

26
Fl. picc.
Ob.
Cl. picc. (Mib)
Fg.
Tr. (Sib)
C. cl.
T. d. B.
senza sord.
avec le pouce
(Лиса выпускаетъ пѣтуха и быстро убѣгаетъ. Пѣтухъ, котъ да баранъ пляшутъ)
(Renard lâche le coq et s'en fuit. Le coq, le chat et le bouc dansent)
(Der Fuchs läßt den Hahn los und entflieht. Hahn, Kater und Bock tanzen einen Freudentanz)
a 3
pizz.
Vl. I, II e Vla
Vlc.
160
come sopra
165

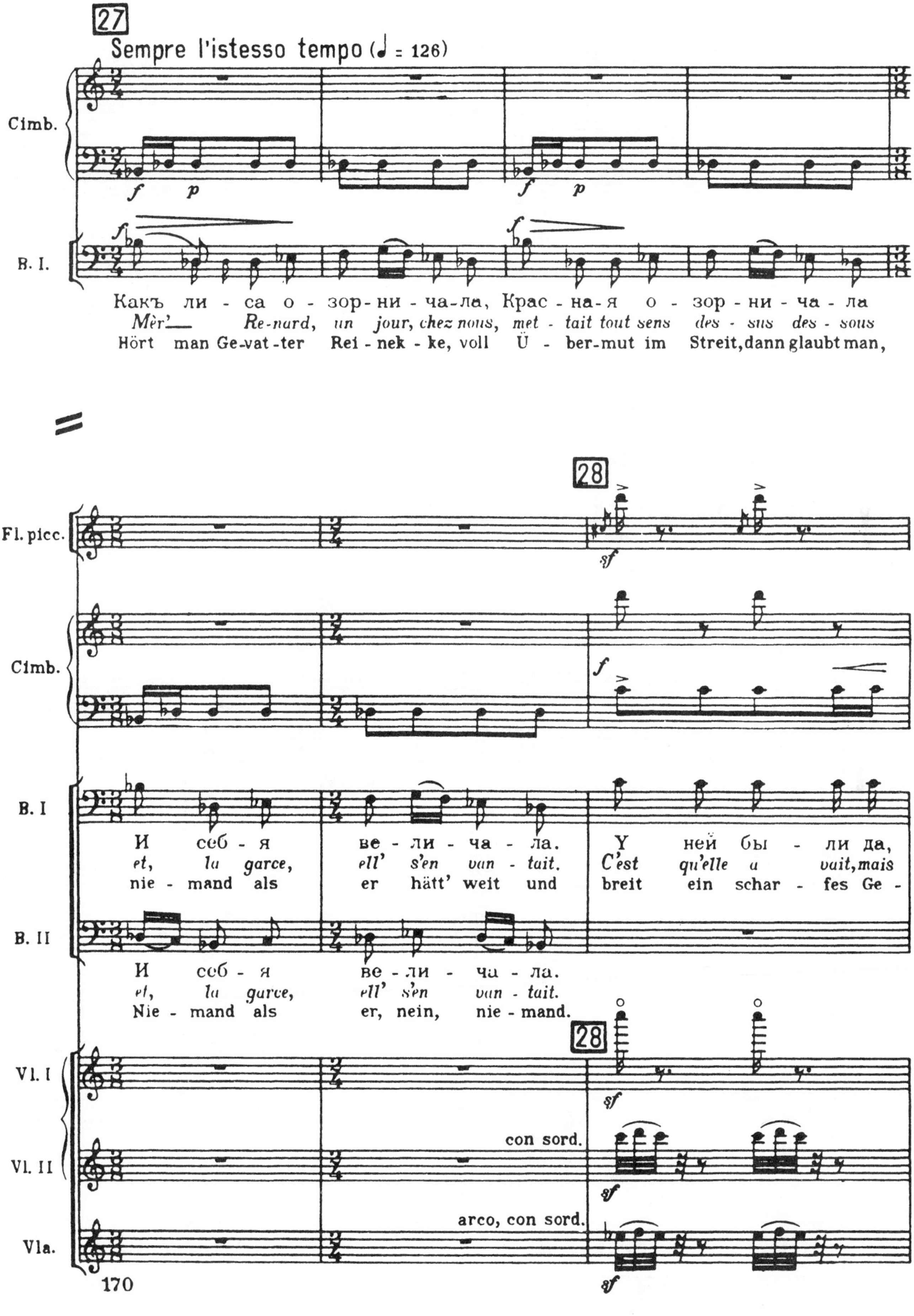

27
Sempre l'istesso tempo (♩ = 126)
Cimb.
B. I.
Какъ ли - са о - зор - ни - ча - ла, Крас - на - я о - зор - ни - ча - ла
Mèr' Re-nard, un jour, chez nous, met - tait tout sens des - sus des - sous
Hört man Ge-vat - ter Rei - nek - ke, voll Ü - ber-mut im Streit, dann glaubt man,

28

Fl. picc.

Cimb.

B. I

И себ - я ве - ли - ча - ла. У ней бы - ли да,
et, la garce, ell' s'en van - tait. C'est qu'elle a vait, mais
nie - mand als er hätt' weit und breit ein schar - fes Ge -

B. II

И себ - я ве - ли - ча - ла.
et, la garce, ell' s'en van - tait.
Nie - mand als er, nein, nie - mand.

28

Vl. I

Vl. II
con sord.

Vla.
arco, con sord.

Fl. picc. = Fl. gr.
Fl. picc.
Cimb.
B. I
у ней бы - ли да, у ней бы - ли да зуб - ки лов - ки да,
c'est qu'elle a vait, mais c'est qu'elle a - vait, pour vous cas -
biß von wei - ßen rie - sen - gro - ßen Zäh-nen gut zum
Vl. I
Vl. II
Vla.
175
29
grazioso
Ob.
con sord.
Cor. (Fa)
Tr. (Sib)
Cimb.
Timp.
B. I
У - сё схва ты - ва - ла го - ло - вки.
ser les reins, un bon ou - til tout prêt.
rei - ßen, zer-flei-schen, würgen, bei - ßen.
arco
Vlc.
Cb.

180
30
Ob.
Cor.
(Fa)
p sub.
p sub.
Tr.
(Sib)
p sub.
Cimb.
subito sf
p
fff
Trgl.
T. d. B.
(à grelots)
f
T. II
Сходилъ кы-не - токъ со дво - ра,
Voi - là m'sieur l'coq qui sort d'chez lui,
Un-ser Gok-kel geht spa - zie - ren
B. I
f
Со дво -
Sort d'chez
Aus dem
B. II
f
Со дво -
Sort d'chez
Aus dem
30
Vlc.
p
sf
Cb.
pizz.
arco
sf
p
180

185
Fl. gr.
mf
Ob.
come sopra
7
Cor. (Fa)
p
Tr. (Sib)
p
Cimb.
fff
Gr. C.
T. II
Сводилъ кы - че - токъ за со - бой
ces dam's pouls sont a - vec lui,
sei - ne Frau - en aus - zu - führen
Ку -
ses
Schön
f
B. I
-ра...
lui,
Haus
За со - бой...
a vec lui,
Er vor - aus.
f
B. II
-ра...
lui,
Haus
За со - бой...
a - vec lui,
Er vor - aus.
f
gliss. pizz. sul Sol
Vl. I
f
gliss. arco sul Sol
Vl. II
f
Vlc.
p
sf
pizz.
arco
Cb.
sf
185
sf
p
sf

31
190
Fl. gr.
Cl. picc. (Mi♭)
Fg.
Cor. (Fa)
Tr. (Si♭)
Cimb.
Timp.
T. I
B. I
B. II
Vl. I
Vl. II
Vlc.
Cb.
- ро - чекъ ря - бу - ше - чекъ.
chèr's p'tit's poul's tach' tées.
ge - fleck - te, bunt - ge - scheck - te.
От - куль...
Tout à coup
Plötz - lich...
От - куль взя - ла -
Tout à coup, (il
Plötz - lich steht an
sim.
pizz.
arco
*) Неопредѣленно низкая нота
Note basse indeterminée

Fg.
Cimb.
Timp.
B. I
От-куль...
Tout à coup
Rei-nek-ke...
Хвостъ под-жа-ла,
mèr' Re-nard
Tief sich nei-gend
B. II
ся ли-си-ца, От-куль взя-ла-ся крас-на-я Хвостъ под-жа-ла,
n'y comptait pas), tout à coup,(il n'y pen-sait pas), mèr' Re-nard
ei-ner Ek-ken, Rei-nek-ke zu al-ler Schrecken. Tief sich nei-gend
Cb.
32
Fg.
cresc.
senza sord.
Cor. (Fa)
Cimb.
senza pedale
Timp.
B. I
Кы-чет-ку че ломъ от-да-ла: „Ча-во шля
est là, ell' vous l'sa-lue tout bas: „Gare à toi, beau
sprichter, höf-lich We-sen zei-gend. „Sag, war-um spa-
B. II
Кы-чет-ку че ломъ от-да-ла.
est là, ell' vous l'sa-lue tout bas.
sprichter, höf-lich We-sen zei-gend.
32
Cb.
195

200
Fg.
ff
1.
Cor. (Fa)
Cimb.
ouvrez peu à peu la pédale
B. I
-ешь-ся, ша-та - ешь-ся? Здѣсь ли-са под - жи-да
gar çon, on t'y prend donc! On va t'don - ner un' bonn'
zierst du g'rad hier mit - ten in des schlau - en Fuch-ses
Vl. I
Vl. II
pizz.
Vla.
f
Vlc.
f
pizz.
Cb.
f
200

33
ossia
205
Fl. gr.
Cl picc. (Mib)
Fg.
Cimb.
Timp.
T. II
„Не ѣшь ме - ня, ли - сынь-
„Ne me mang' pas, mèr' Re -
„Friß mich nicht, ich bit - te
B. I
етъ - мяс - ца."
p'tit' le - çon!"
Jagd - re - vier?"
33
Vl. I
Vl. II
arco
Vla.
Vlc.
arco
Cb.
205
ossia

ossia
210
Fl. gr.
Cl. picc. (Mib)
Fg.
Cimb.
T. I
ка,
nard,
dich!
B. I
Не
ѣшь
ме
ня,
mèr'
Re
nard,
pi
Hör'
mein
Fle
hen,
Vl. I
sempre sim.
Vl. II
Vla.
Vlc.
Cb.
210

34
215
ossia
Fl. gr.
Cl. picc. (Mi♭)
Cimb.
B. I
кра - сна я! Не бу-детъ ли съ теб-я Ку-
tié pour moi! N'au-ras tu pas as-sez a-
scho - ne mich! Nimm von den schön-ge-fleck-ten
B. II
Ку-
a-
von
34
Vl. I
Vl. II
Vla.
Vlc.
Cb.
215

*) En cas d'absence du *Ré* grave / Falls das tiefe *D* fehlt
**) parlando (*mezza voce*)

220
Fl. gr.
Cl. picc. (Mi♭)
Tr. (Si♭)
Cimb.
sim.
C. cl.
T. I
- - - чу мя - - - сца ин - - на - го,
ta car - cass' qu'il me faut.
Freund, mein Ge - schmack ist ein - - mal so,
Vl. II
Vla.
Vlc.
Cb.
220

ossia
225
Fl. gr. = Fl. picc.
36
Fl. gr.
Ob.
Cl. picc. (Mib)
Cl. picc. in Mib = Cl. in La
Tr. (Sib)
Cimb.
C. cl.
p
T. I.
f
Хо - чу пѣ - ту - ши - на - го!"
J'au - rai ta peau, j'au - rai tes os!"
such' mir ein Hähn-chen zum Ri - sot - to!"
36
Vl. II
Vla.
Vlc.
Cb.
225

230
Ob.
Fg.
con sord.
Tr. (Si♭)
mp
C. cl.
T. I
f
B. I
O
O
o
Vl. II
Vla.
Vlc.
Cb.
230

37
235
come sopra
Ob.
Fg.
staccato
Tr.
(Si♭)
C. cl.
T. I
molto
B. I
Vl. II
Vla.
Vlc.
Cb.
235

240
Ob.
Fg.
come sopra
Tr. (Sib)
come sopra
7
7
C. cl.
T. I
molto
T. II
B. I
come sopra
B. II
come sopra
Vl. II
Vla.
Vlc.
Cb.
240

38
245
Ob.
Fg.
Tr.
(Sib)
C. cl.
cresc.
come sopra
T. I
come sopra
T. II
molto
molto
B. I
B. II
38
Vl. II
Vla.
Vle.
Cb.
245

39
Ob. = Cor. ingl.
Ob.
Fg.
Tr. (Sib)
Cimb.
Ped.
Timp.
f secco
C. cl.
T. I
T. II
B. I
Взяла ли - са
Voi-là qu'mèr Re-
Schon hat ihn
B. II
Взяла ли - са
Voi-là qu'mèr Re -
Schon hat ihn
39
avec le talon
stacc. e cresc.
Vl. I
Vl. II
Vla.
Vlc.
Cb.

Cimb.
senza Ped.
Ped.
simile
senza Ped.
Timp.
B. I
кы - че - та за_бо - ки,
nard prend l'coq par - les côt's,
Rei - nek - ke beim Kra - gen.
По - не - сла е - го да - лё - ко -
ell' saut' d'un bond l'mur, ell_saut' l'aug',
Ei - lends wird er fort - ge - tra - gen,
B. II
По - не - сла...
ell' saut'
Ei - lends wird...
Vl. I
Vl. II
Vla.
250
Fl. picc.
Fl. picc. = Fl. gr.
Cimb.
senza Ped.
Ped.
senza Ped.
Timp.
B. I
(B. II)
За пень, за_ко - ло - ду,
l'tir' par lu_peau du dos,
(I) ü - ber Stock und ü - ber
За бѣ - лу - ю бе - ре - зу...
l'em port'der - rièr' le bou - leau...
Stein, hinter'm weißen Zaun. (Basso II) Er -
Vl. I
Vl. II
pizz.
Vla.
Vlc.
Cb.
255

Fl. picc.
Cimb.
Timp.
Ped.
(Котъ да баранъ удаляются)
(Le chat et le bouc se retirent)
(Kater und Bock ziehen sich zurück)
B. I
Ку - ры кы-че-та не слы-шутъ
Ces dam's sont trop loin, ell's n'en tend't rien.
Niemand hört ihn, niemand hilft ihm.
B. II
Кы-четъ кличетъ да кы-четъ кличетъ... Ку - ры кы-че-та не слы-шутъ
Co - co - co - co - co - coq, pauv' coq! Ces dam's sont trop loin, ell's n'en tend't rien.
tönt sein jäm-mer-lich Hil - fe - schrein. Niemand hört ihn, niemand hilft ihm.
40
Vl. I
Vl. II
arco
Vla.
pizz.
gliss. sul Do
41
Meno mosso (♩ = 63)
Cor. ingl.
Fg.
Cor. (Fa)
Cimb.
Gr. C.
(Пѣтухъ взбирается на свою вышку и усаживается поудобнѣе)
(Le coq remonte sur son perchoir et s'installe commodément)
(Der Hahn besteigt seinen Sitz und macht es sich bequem)
41
Meno mosso (♩ = 63)
Vla.
pizz.
poco sf
260

42
con sord.
Tr. (Si♭)
pp
T. I
42
Си-жу на ду - бу,
Je suis sur mon bâ-ton,
Von mei-ner War-te aus
Си - жу,домъ стере-гу,
je garde la mai-son,
sing' ich in al-le Welt
arco sul do
sempre simile
sempre simile
pizz.
Vlc.
Cb.
265
Cor. ingl.
Cor. ingl. = Oboe
Fg.
Cor. (Fa)
Tr. (Si♭)
Cimb.
(Приходитъ лиса.
Она сбрасываетъ съ себя
монашеское одѣяніе)
T. I
Пѣс - ню по ю.
j'chante ma chan-son.
hin-aus, ich wahr'dies Haus.
(Arrive Renard. Il laisse tomber son costume de religieuse)
(Der Fuchs erscheint, er läßt das Mönchskleid fallen)
Vlc.
pizz.
sf
Cb.
270

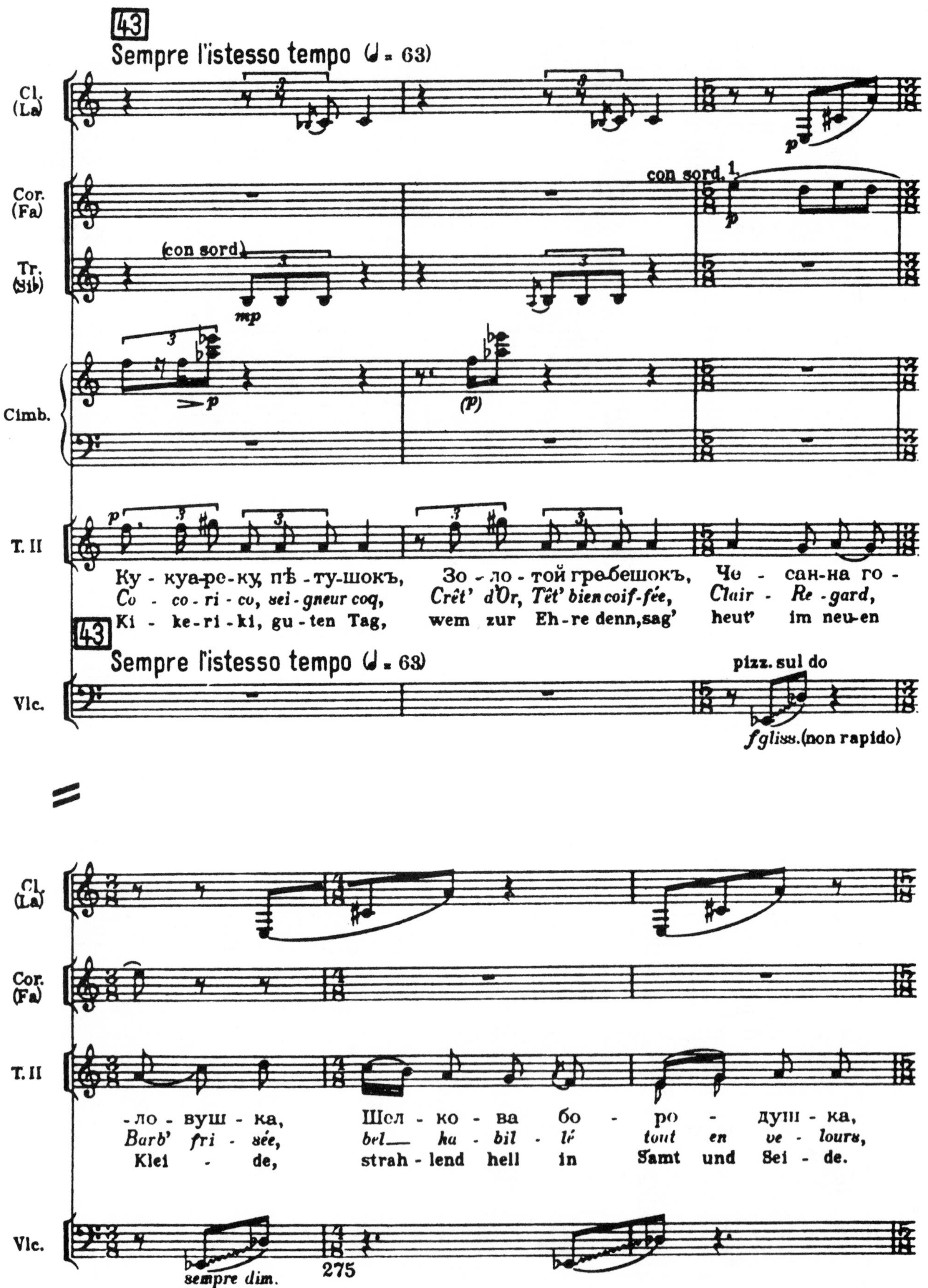
43
Sempre l'istesso tempo (♩ = 63)
Cl. (La)
Cor. (Fa)
con sord. 1
Tr. (Si♭)
(con sord.)
mp
Cimb.
p
(p)
T. II
Ку - куа-ре-ку, пѣ - ту-шокъ, Зо - ло - той гребешокъ, Че - сан-на го -
Co - co-ri-co, sei-gneur coq, Crêt' d'Or, Têt' bien coif-fée, Clair - Re-gard,
Ki - ke-ri-ki, gu-ten Tag, wem zur Eh-re denn, sag' heut' im neu-en
43
Sempre l'istesso tempo (♩ = 63)
Vlc.
pizz. sul do
f gliss. (non rapido)
Cl. (La)
Cor. (Fa)
T. II
- ло - вуш - ка, Шел - ко - ва бо - ро - душ - ка,
Barb' fri - sée, bel___ ha - bil - lé tout en ve - lours,
Klei - de, strah - lend hell in Samt und Sei - de.
Vlc.
sempre dim.
275

44
Fl. gr.
Cl. (La)
T. I
T. II
Vlc.
mf
Не гля - жу въо -
Non, je n't'ou - vri -
Fällt mir nicht im
Вы - гля - ни въо - кош - ко.
beau sei - gneur coq, ouvr' moi.
Zeig' dich doch am Fen - ster - lein.
44
Fl. gr.
Cl. (La)
Cor. (Fa)
T. I
T. II
Vlc.
1.
- кош - ко. Не на - до мнѣ го - ро - шку.
rai pas. Les coqs n'aiment pas les p'tits pois,
Trau - me ein. Be - dau - re, brau - che kei - ne.
Дамъ теб - ѣ го - ро - шку.
J'te donn'rai des p'tits pois.
Sieh doch, Erbsen, fei - ne.
280

45
Cl. (La)
Fg.
Tr. (Si♭)
T. I
Vla.
Vlc.
poco sf
arco
mf
Пѣ-тухъ ка - шку ку - ша - етъ, ли - су не - слу - ша
les coqs aiment seul'-ment le grain, Re - nard parle ils_ n'en-tend'nt
Laß mich mit_ der-lei_ in Ruh', hab' all' das_ bes-ser als
285
Fl. gr.
Ob.
Cor. (Fa)
B. I
Vl. I
Vl. II
Cb.
trem.
1. senza sord.
-етъ. rien. du.
(Фальцетъ) (fausset) (Falsett)
Пѣ - ту - шокъ,__ пѣ - ту - шокъ!
Pe - tit coq,__ pe - tit_ coq,
Hab' noch mehr, o, hab' noch mehr,
pizz.
f
(sempre simile)
con sord.
arco
290

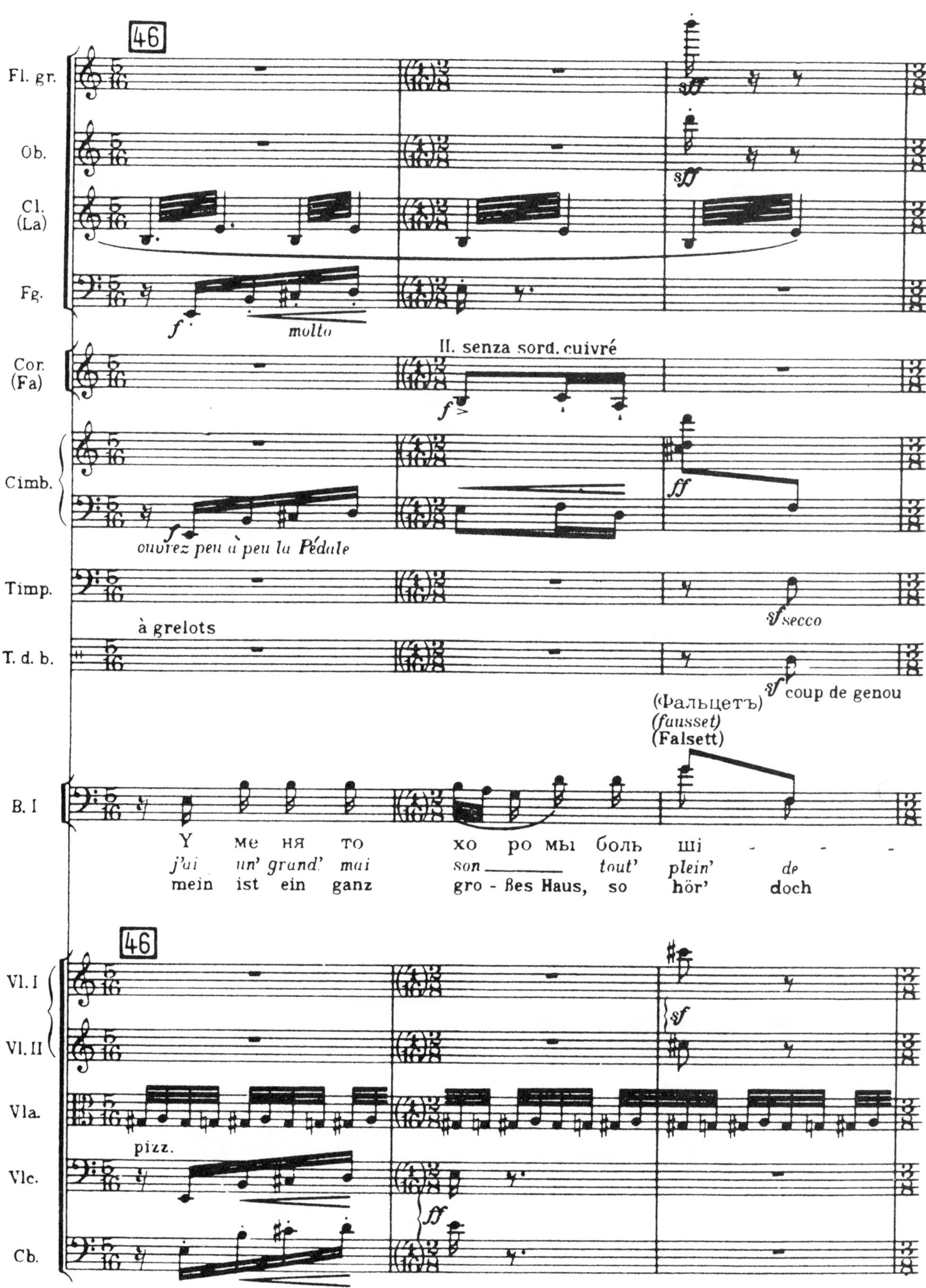
46
Fl. gr.
Ob.
Cl. (La)
Fg.
molto
Cor. (Fa)
II. senza sord. cuivré
Cimb.
ouvrez peu à peu la Pédale
Timp.
secco
à grelots
T. d. b.
coup de genou
(Фальцетъ)
(fausset)
(Falsett)
B. I
У ме ня то хо ро мы боль ші
j'ai un' grand' mai son tout' plein' de
mein ist ein ganz gro - ßes Haus, so hör' doch
46
Vl. I
Vl. II
Vla.
pizz.
Vlc.
Cb.

295
Cl. (La)
Fg.
come sopra
Cimb.
Gr. C.
mf
B. I
e,
grain,
her.
Въ каждомъ у-глу
tu en au-rus
Je - des Eck-chen
Vl. I
Vl. II
Vla.
Vlc.
arco
ff
pizz.
Cb.
ff
295

47
Fl.gr.
Ob.
Cl. (La)
Fg.
Cor. (Fa)
come sopra
Cimb.
Timp.
Gr. C.
à grelots
T.d.b.
simile
(Фальцетъ)
(fausset)
(Falsett)
B. I
пшенич ки - по мѣ - роч - кѣ:
tant que tu vou d'ras...
voll von Wei - zen, kei - nes leer,
47
Vl. I
Vl. II
Vla.
arco
Vlc.
Cb.

*) Исполнять такъ: сыт-(та) не-хо - чу.

**) *Pour le française et l'allemand cette fin de la phrase est confiée au 1er tenor, la basse se taisant.*

**) Im Französischen und Deutschen wird das Ende des Satzes vom 1. Tenor gesungen, während der Baß pausiert.

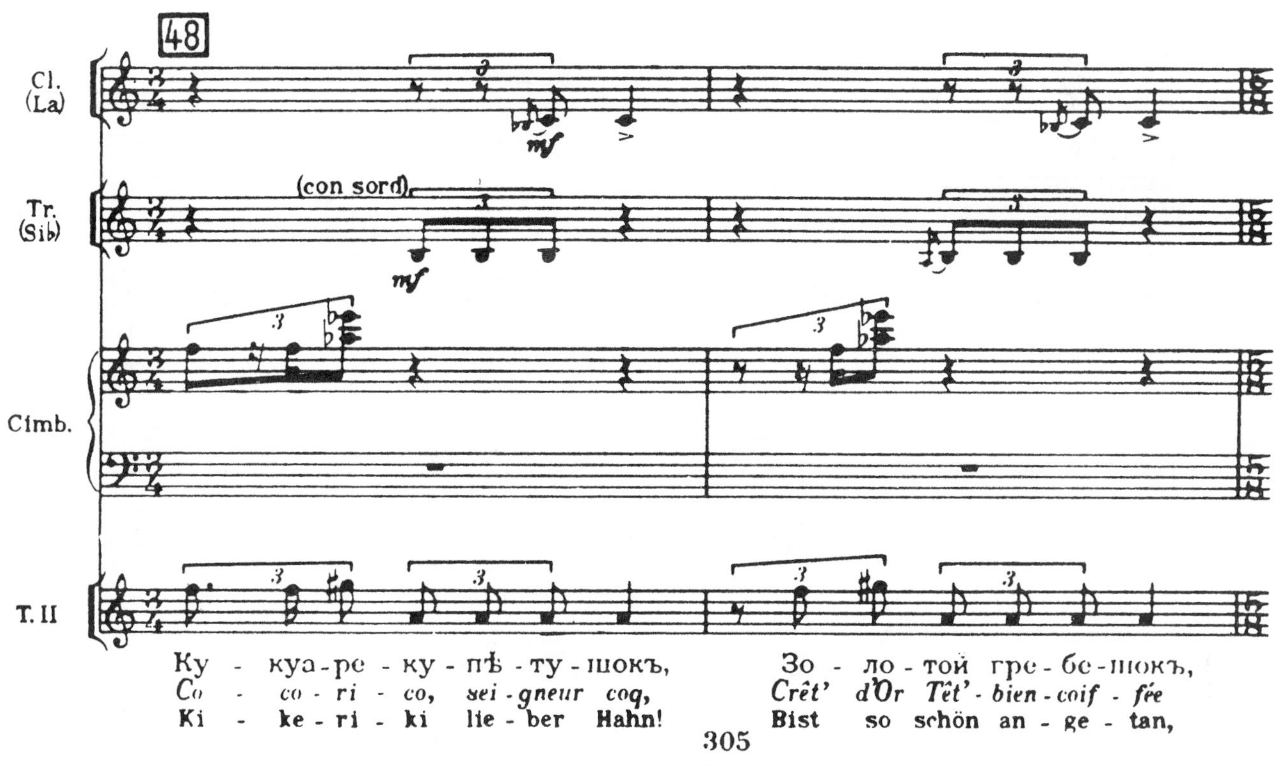
48
Cl. (La)
(con sord)
Tr. (Sib)
Cimb.
T. II
Ку - куа-ре - ку-пѣ - ту - шокъ, Зо - ло - той гре-бе-шокъ,
Co - co-ri - co, sei-gneur coq, Crêt' d'Or Têt' - bien-coif - fée
Ki - ke-ri - ki lie - ber Hahn! Bist so schön an - ge - tan,
305

come sopra
Cl. (La)
T. II
Шел - ко - ва бо - ро - ду - шка! Вы - гля - ни въ о -
Clair - Re - gard, — Barb' - fri - sée, beau sei - gneur coq,
scha - de, daß ich nur von weit' se - hen kann dein
arco
Vl. I
dolce
pizz. come sopra
Vlc.
gliss.

Cl. (La)
Cor. (Fa)
1. con sord.
T. I
Не
M'en -
Magst
T. II
кош - ко, Дамъ те - бѣ ле - пё - шку.
ouvr' moi; j't'ap - port' un mor - ceau d'pain.
rei - ches Kleid. Hab' ganz fri - schen Ku - - chen.
Vl. I
Vlc.
310
49
Fl. gr.
Cl. (La)
Cor. (Fa)
1.
Tr. (Sib)
(con sord.)
poco sf
T. I
на до мнѣ ле - пе - шки Пѣ - тухъ
nuie pas a - vec ton pain! Pas si
ihn al - lein ver - - su - chen! Bin doch
49
senza sord.
Vla.
mf
Vlc.

315
Cl.
(La)
Fg.
mf
Tr.
(Si♭)
Cimb.
5
T. I
не такъ то глупъ, Не гло - дать - те - бѣ_ мой
bêt', pas_ si bêt'! Je gard' mon bien, gard' ton
nicht gar_ so dumm, du_ kriegst mich nicht her -
Vl. I
Vl. II
Vla.
Vlc.
Cb.
315

50
Fl. gr.
Ob.
Cl. (La)
Fg.
Cor. (Fa)
Tr. (Sib)
Cimb.
Ptti.
Trgl.
T. I
B. I
1. con sord.
f senza Ped.
etouffez
baguette en bois
хлупъ.
bien.
um.
(Фальцетъ)
(fausset)
(Falsett)
Охъ, ты пѣ -
Coq de mon
Hör' doch, lie - bes
50
Vl. I
Vl. II
Vla.
Vlc.
Cb.
pizz.
(pizz.)
con sord.
arco

320
Fl. gr.
Ob.
Cl. (La)
Fg.
Cor. (Fa)
bouché cuivré
Cimb.
ouvrez peu à peu la Ped.
Timp.
sf secco
Trgl.
T. d. b.
à grelots sf
coup de genou
B. I
тя, пѣ - ту— шокъ, Спу-щайся ка ты на ни - зя - ще -
coeur, beau pe-tit coq, des cends d'où tu es perché vers plus
Hähn - chen, be-ster Freund, kommet-was nä-her, ach so hör' mich
B. II
...ще -
...plus
mich
Vl. I
Vl. II
Vla.
Vlc.
pizz.
Cb.
molto
320

325
Fl. gr.
Ob.
Cl. (La)
Fg.
Cor. (Fa)
come sopra
Cimb.
Timp.
Gr. C.
T. d. b.
come sopra
(Фальцетъ)
(fausset)
(Falsett)
B. I
- е, Съ ни-зя - ща-го на зем - ля - ще -
bas, et d'en cor' plus bas jusqu' sur la
doch, Bis zur Er - de bißchen tie - fer
B. II
- е, ...ще -
bas, ...la
doch. ...fer
Vl. I
Vl. II
Vla.
arco
pizz.
Vlc.
Cb.
325

51
Fl. gr.
Ob.
Cl. (La)
Cor. (Fa)
Cimb.
Gr. C.
B. I
-e,
terre,
noch.
Я тво - ю ду -
Et je t'em - port' -
Will zum Dank dich
B. II
-e.
terre,
noch.
51
Vl. I
Vl. II
Vla.
arco
Vlc.
pizz.
ff
Cb.
ff

330
Fl. gr.
sff
Ob.
sff
Cl. (La)
1.
Cor. (Fa)
Cimb.
sff
Timp.
Gr. C.
come sopra
T. d. B.
à grelots
(Фальцетъ)
(fausset) (Falset)
B. I
-шгу на не-бе - са взне - су!
rai tout vi-vant dans le ciel.
tra-gen bis zum Him - mel hoch.
B. II
...взне - су!
...le ciel.
...mel hoch.
Vl. I
Vl. II
Vla.
arco
Vlc.
sff
Cb.
830
sff

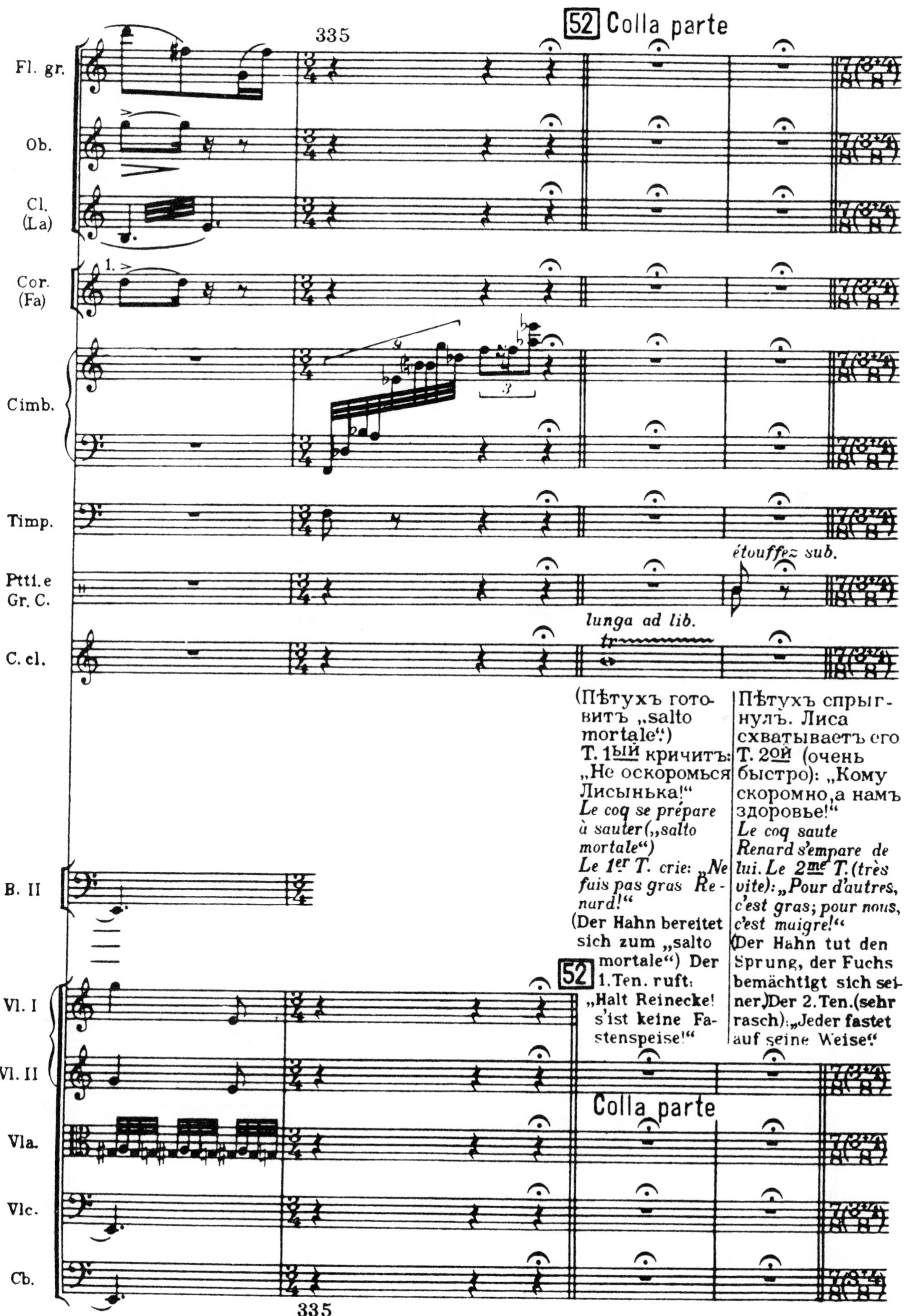

335
52 Colla parte
Fl. gr.
Ob.
Cl. (La)
Cor. (Fa)
1.
Cimb.
3
Timp.
étouffez sub.
Ptti. e Gr. C.
lunga ad lib.
tr
C. cl.
(Пѣтухъ готовитъ „salto mortale“.)
Т. 1ый кричитъ: „Не оскоромься Лисынька!“
Le coq se prépare à sauter („salto mortale“)
Le 1er T. crie: „Ne fais pas gras Renard!“
(Der Hahn bereitet sich zum „salto mortale“) Der 1. Ten. ruft: „Halt Reinecke! s'ist keine Fastenspeise!“
Пѣтухъ спрыгнулъ. Лиса схватываетъ его Т. 2ой (очень быстро): „Кому скоромно, а намъ здоровье!“
Le coq saute Renard s'empare de lui. Le 2me T. (très vite): „Pour d'autres, c'est gras; pour nous, c'est maigre!“
(Der Hahn tut den Sprung, der Fuchs bemächtigt sich seiner.) Der 2. Ten. (sehr rasch): „Jeder fastet auf seine Weise“.
B. II
52
Vl. I
Vl. II
Colla parte
Vla.
Vlc.
Cb.
335

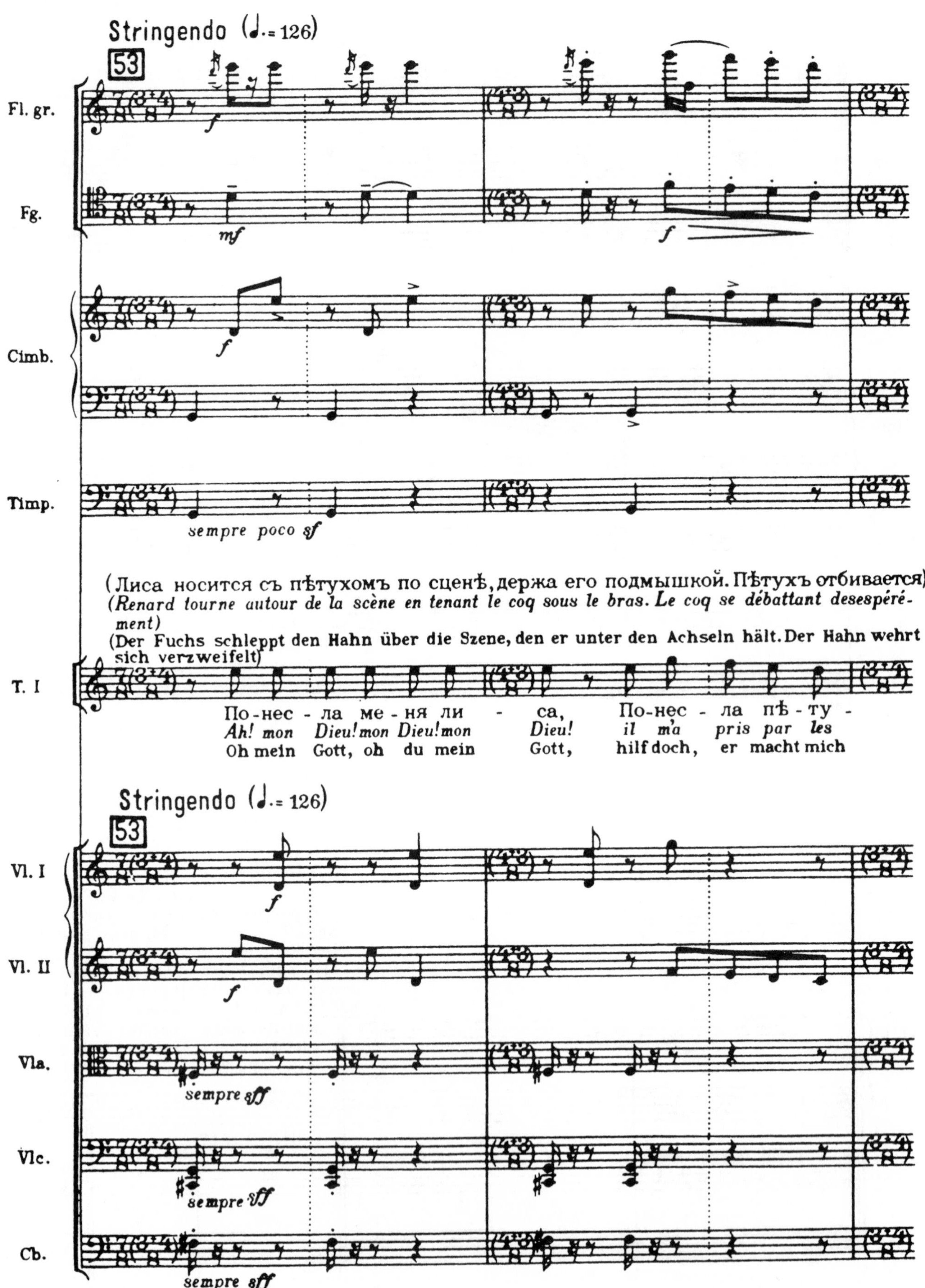

Stringendo (♩. = 126)
53
Fl. gr.
Fg.
Cimb.
Timp.
sempre poco sf
(Лиса носится съ пѣтухомъ по сценѣ, держа его подмышкой. Пѣтухъ отбивается)
(Renard tourne autour de la scène en tenant le coq sous le bras. Le coq se débattant desespérément)
(Der Fuchs schleppt den Hahn über die Szene, den er unter den Achseln hält. Der Hahn wehrt sich verzweifelt)
T. I
По-нес - ла ме - ня ли - са, По-нес - ла пѣ - ту -
Ah! mon Dieu! mon Dieu! mon Dieu! il m'a pris par les
Oh mein Gott, oh du mein Gott, hilf doch, er macht mich
Stringendo (♩. = 126)
53
Vl. I
Vl. II
Vla.
sempre sff
Vlc.
sempre sff
Cb.
sempre sff

340
Fl. gr.
come sopra
Fg.
mf
f
Cimb.
Timp.
T. I
- ха, По кру-тымъ бе-реж - камъ, По вы - сокимъ го -
ch'veux, il m'a pris par les ch'veux, il me tir' par la
tot, er zerrt mich, zer-beißt mich, er zer - fetzt und zer -
Vl. I
Vl. II
Vla.
Vlc.
Cb.
340

54
Fl. gr.
Fg.
con sord.
Tr. (Si♭)
sf
sf
Cimb.
Timp.
T. I
-рамъ,Въ чу-жi - я зем - ли, Въ да - ле - кi - я страны,
queue, il va m'mettr' tout nu comm' un pe - tit Jé - sus
reißt mich, mein schö - nes Kleid, mein schö - nes Fe - der-kleid,
54
Vl. I
Vl. II
Vla.
Vlc.
Cb.

Fl. gr.
Cl. (La)
Fg.
Cor. (Fa)
non f e non cresc.
Tr. (Sib)
sf
Cimb.
Timp.
T. I.
За три - де - вять зе - мель, Въ тридла - то - е царство, Въ триде-
j'suis per - du, j'suis fi - chu, au s'cours j'en peux plus, ah! mon Dieu,
und ver-schleppt mich so weit, so weit — von hier. Hat denn kei - ner
arco
Vl. I
Vl. II
(arco) sul do
Vla.
345
Tr. (Sib)
(a 3)
sf
Cimb.
T. I.
- ся - - то - - е го су - дар - ство;
qui l'au rait cru, qui l'au - rait cru?...
Mit - - leid, Mit - leid mit mir?

55
Fl. gr.
Ob.
Cl. (La)
Fg.
Cor. (Fa)
senza sord.
Tr. (Si♭)
Cimb.
ff
*)
Timp.
f
T. I
f
Котъ да ба-ранъ, Хо четъ съѣсть ме-ня ли-са!
Frèr' bouc, frèr' chat, pour quoi n'êt's vous pas là?
Barm - her - zig - keit, Böck-chen, Ka - ter - chen, Brüderlein,
55
arco
pizz.
arco
pizz.
Vl. I
ff
sempre sim.
arco
pizz.
arco
pizz.
Vl. II
ff
sempre sim.
arco
pizz.
arco
pizz.
Vla.
ff
sempre sim.
Vlc.
ff
Cb.
ff
trem.
*) Pour l'instrument qui possède le ré grave exécuter:
Das Instrument mit dem tiefen d spielt:

350
Fl. gr.
Ob.
Cl.
(La)
Fg.
Cor.
(Fa)
Tr.
(Sib)
Cimb.
*)
Timp.
T. I
Котъ да ба ранъ,
frèr' bouc, frèr chat,
Barm - her - zig - keit,
Хо четъ съѣсть пѣ ту ха!
bons a - mis, e - cou - tez moi,
e - wig will ich euch dankbar sein
arco
pizz.
Vl. I
Vl. II
Vla.
Vlc.
Cb.
350

*) come sopra

56
𝅝 = 𝅗𝅥. (♩ = 84)
(♩. = 84)
Fl. gr.
Ob.
Oboe = Cor. ingl.
Cl. (La)
Fg.
Cor. (Fa)
marc.
Tr. (Sib)
Cimb.
*)
Timp.
T. I
Котъ да - ба - ранъ, О ты-ми - те ме - ня!
frèr' bouc, frèr' chat, c'en est fait d'moi cett' fois!
in E - wig - keit, werd' ich durch euch be - freit!
T. II
О ты-ми - те ме - ня!
c'en est fait d'moi cett' fois!
... werd' ich durch euch be - freit!
arco
pizz.
Vl. I
Vl. II
Vla.
Vlc.
Cb.

*) come sopra

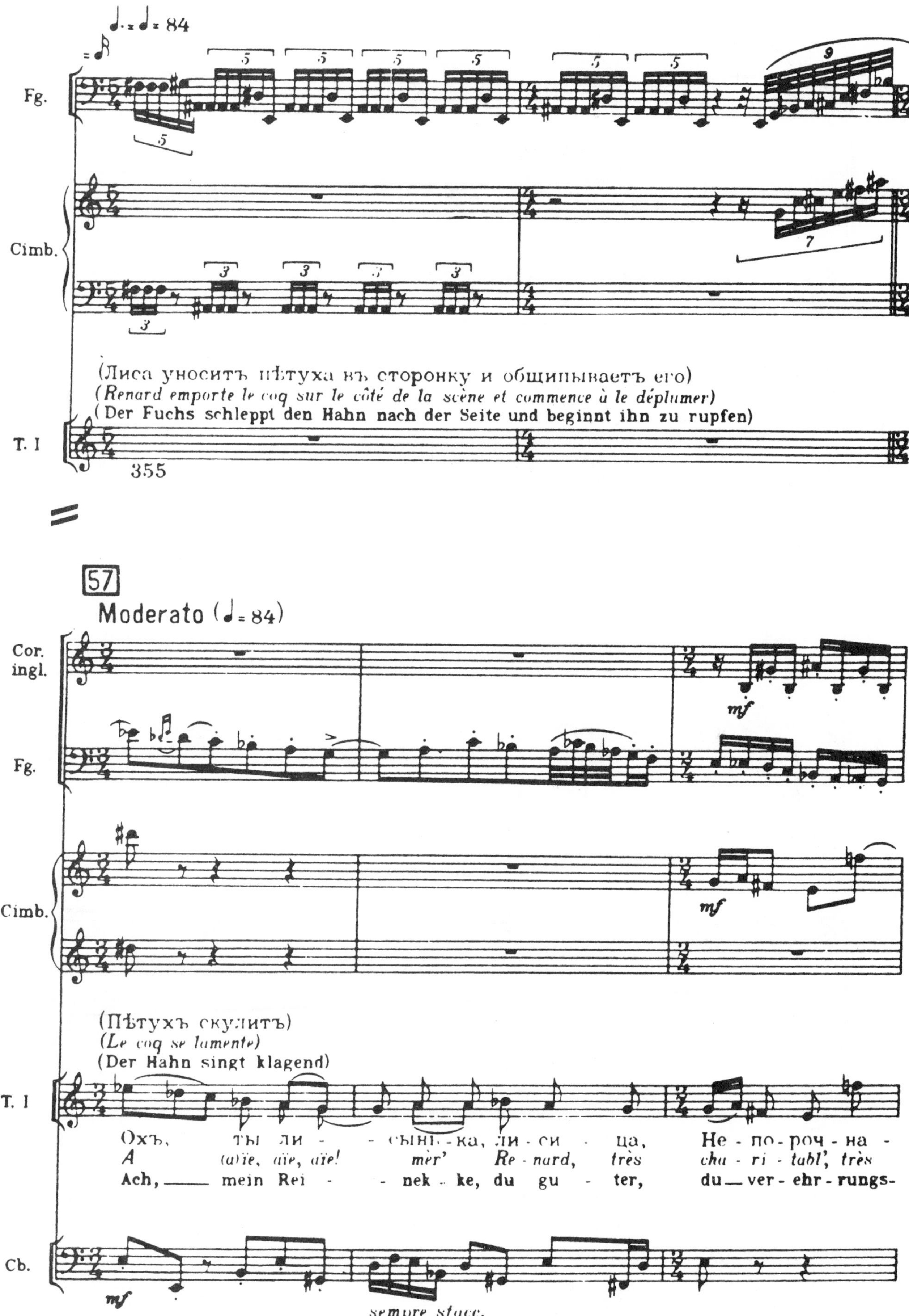
Fg.
Cimb.
(Лиса уноситъ пѣтуха въ сторонку и общипываетъ его)
(Renard emporte le coq sur le côté de la scène et commence à le déplumer)
(Der Fuchs schleppt den Hahn nach der Seite und beginnt ihn zu rupfen)
T. I
355
57
Moderato
Cor. ingl.
mf
Fg.
Cimb.
mf
(Пѣтухъ скулитъ)
(Le coq se lamente)
(Der Hahn singt klagend)
T. I
Охъ, ты ли - сынь-ка, ли-си - ца, Не-по-роч-на -
A (a)ïe, aïe, aïe! mèr' Re-nard, très cha-ri-tabl', très
Ach, mein Rei - nek - ke, du gu - ter, du ver-ehr-rungs-
Cb.
mf
sempre stacc.

360
58
Cor. ingl.
Fg.
Cor. (Fa)
mf en dehors
Cimb.
p
f étouffez
(senza Ped.)
secco
Timp.
f
T. I
я сес-три-ца! Какъ у на-ше-го, у ба - - - -
vé - né - ra - ble, viens chez pa - pa, et
würd'ger Bru-der, sieh', in mei-nes lie - ben Va - - - - ters
58
arco
Vl. I
mf
p
arco
Vl. II
mf
p
pizz.
arco
Vla.
mf
p
secco
pizz.
arco
Vlc.
sff
sf
mf
p
Cb.
360

365
Cor. ingl.
Cl. (La)
Fg.
Cor. (Fa)
dim.
dim.
Cimb.
come sopra
Timp.
T. I
тюш - ки ма - - - - сли - цемъ блинки по - ли - -
tu ver - ras, là bas chez pa - pa, tu ver - -
Hau - se längst er-war-ten al - le dich zum Schmau-se,
pizz.
Vla.
secco
pizz.
Vlc.
Cb.
365

Cor. ingl.
Cl. (La)
Fg.
Cor. (Fa)
Timp.
T. I
-ва - ють те-бя въ го - сти под-жи-да - - ють.
-ras, comme on te soign' - ra, tu ver - ras, comm'
reich be - setzt die Ta - fel, reich-lich fein Ge - tränk,
Vla.
pizz.
sf
Vlc.
arco secco
pizz.
sf
Cb.

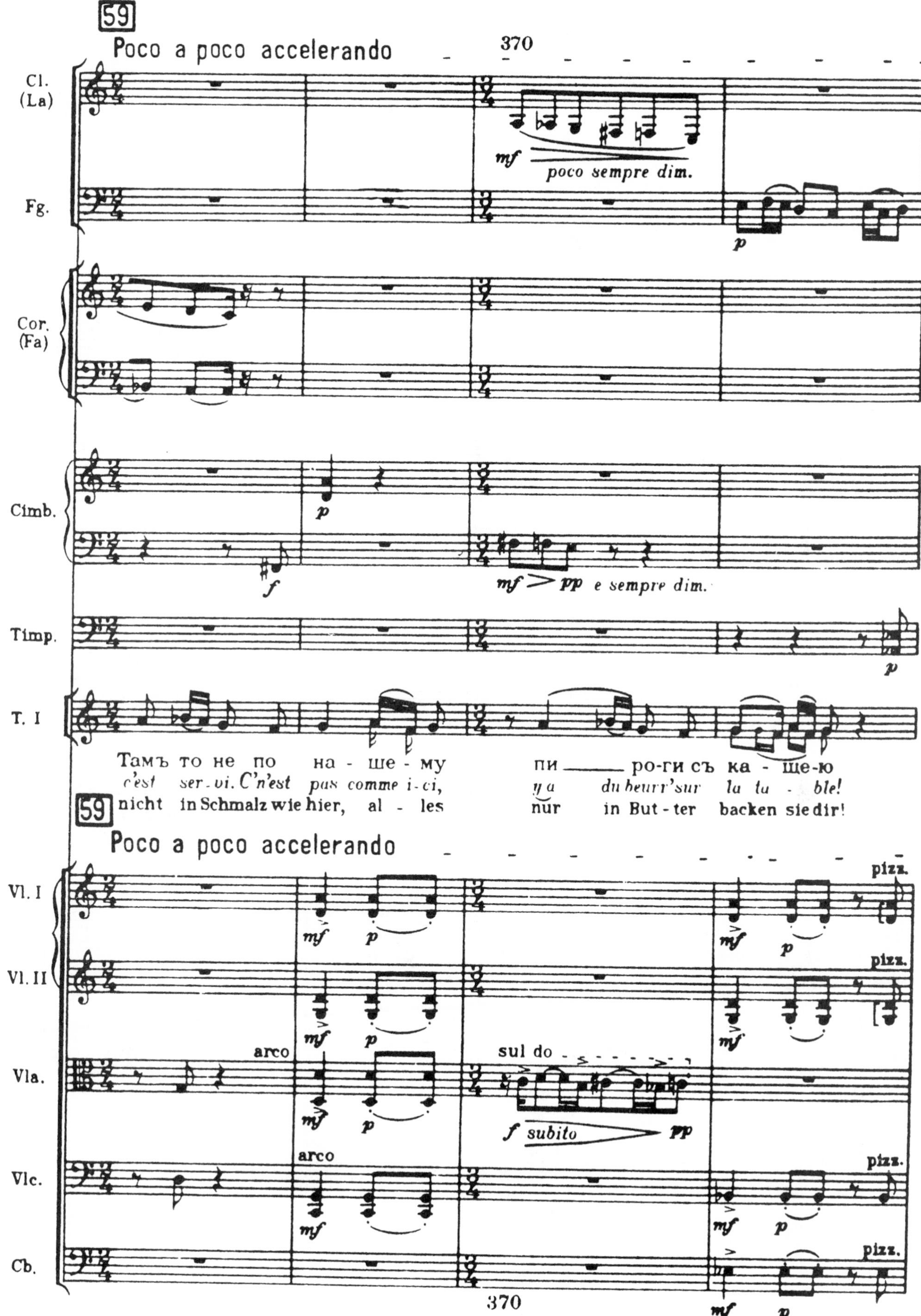
59
Poco a poco accelerando
370
Cl.
(La)
poco sempre dim.
Fg.
Cor.
(Fa)
Cimb.
e sempre dim.
Timp.
T. I
Тамъ то не по на - ше - му пи — ро-ги съ ка - ще-ю
c'est ser-vi. C'n'est pas comme i-ci, y a du beurr' sur la ta - ble!
nicht in Schmalz wie hier, al - les nur in But-ter backen sie dir!
59
Poco a poco accelerando
Vl. I
pizz.
Vl. II
pizz.
arco
sul do
Vla.
f subito
Vlc.
arco
pizz.
Cb.
pizz.
370

al ♩= 112
60
375
Cl. (La)
Cimb.
T. I
По - мя - ни, Гос-по-ди Си - - - до - ра, Ма -
Sei - gneur, prends sous ta gard' Sé - - - ra - phi - ne,
Herr Gott, er - barm'dich, er - hö - re mich, laß
Vl. I
Vl. II
Vla.
Vlc.
Cb.
arco
sul do
come sopra
mf p
ff pp
375

Fl. gr.
Cor. ingl.
Cl. (La)
Fg.
Cor. (Fa)
Tr. (Si♭)
Timp.
sempre p
T. I
-ка - ра, Треть-я - го За - ха - ра,Трехъ Ма -
ma cou - sin', ma bonn' mar - rain' Cath'rine, tous les
dei - ner Huld emp-foh-len sein mein Müt - - ter -
Vl. I
Vl. II
Vla.
Vlc.
Cb.
pizz.

380
61
Fl. gr.
Cor. ingl.
Cl. (La)
Fg.
Cor. (Fa)
Tr. (Sib)
Timp.
sempre p
T. I
p
-тренъ, Да Лу-кусъ Пет-ромъ, Дѣ - да Ми-ро-ѣ -
Saints, An - dré mon par-rain, A - de-lin' qui fait l'pain,
lein, ja mein Müt-ter-lein, laß al-le sie
61
Vl. I
Vl. II
Vla.
Vlc.
Cb.
arco
pizz.
mf
p
380

Fl. gr.
Cor. ingl.
Cl. (La)
Fg.
Cor. ingl. = Oboe
ppp
Cor. (Fa)
con sord: pp
Tr. (Si♭)
con sord.
pp
Timp.
T. I
— да, Ба - бку Бѣльма - тку, Тю шу да — Ка-тю-шу, Ба - буш -
— et Jean qui tra-vaille au — mou-lin, Fé - li cie, Fe - li - ci(e Si) do
— in dei - nen Himmel ein, Ma-rie, Kath'rin — und Pe - ter, mei - nen
Vl. I
Vl. II
Vla.
Vlc.
Cb.
arco
pizz.

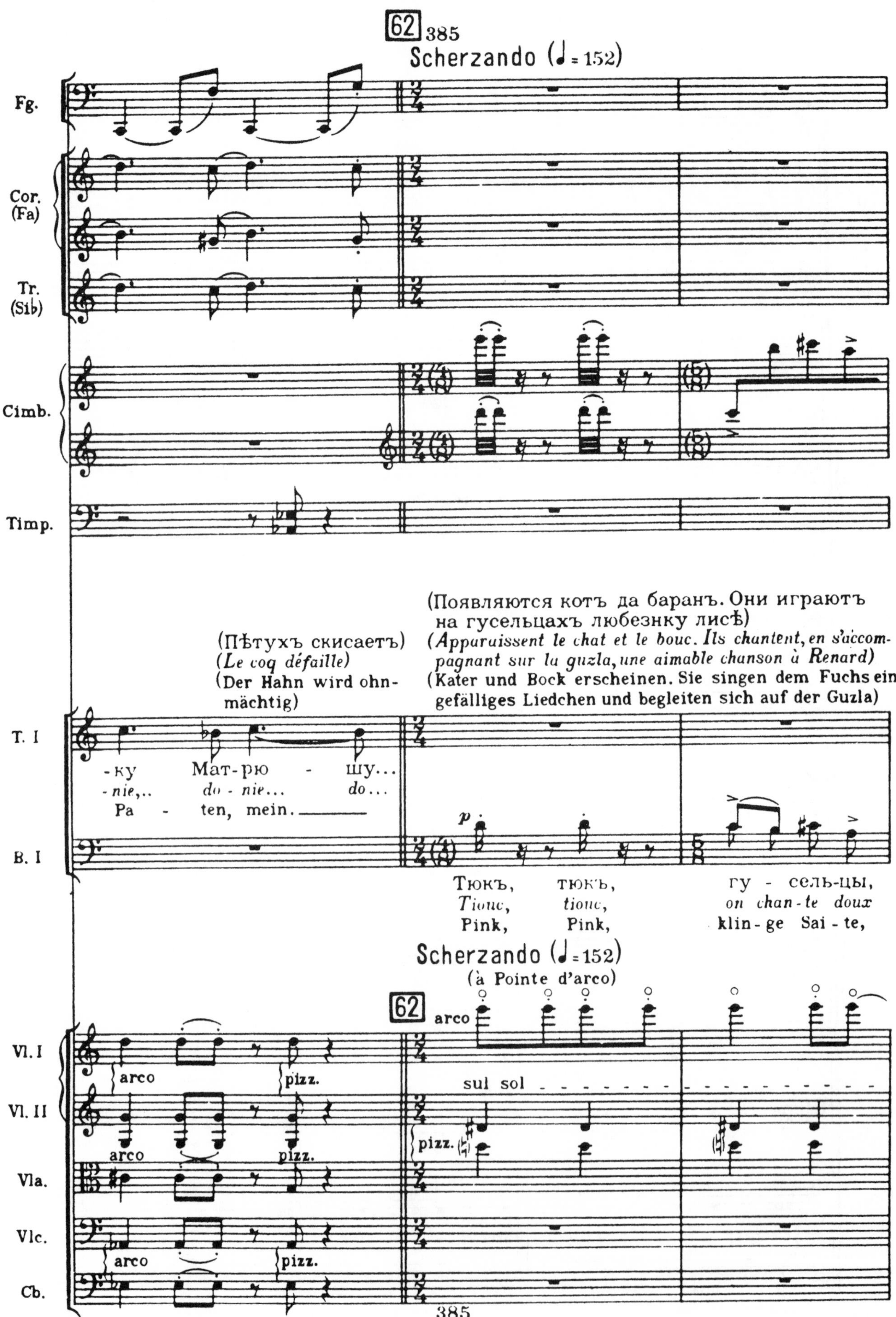
62 385
Scherzando (♩= 152)
Fg.
Cor. (Fa)
Tr. (Sib)
Cimb.
Timp.
(Пѣтухъ скисаетъ)
(Le coq défaille)
(Der Hahn wird ohnmächtig)
(Появляются котъ да баранъ. Они играютъ на гусельцахъ любезнку лисѣ)
(Apparaissent le chat et le bouc. Ils chantent, en s'accompagnant sur la guzla, une aimable chanson à Renard)
(Kater und Bock erscheinen. Sie singen dem Fuchs ein gefälliges Liedchen und begleiten sich auf der Guzla)
T. I
-ку Мат-рю - шу...
-nie,.. do - nie... do...
Pa - ten, mein.
B. I
p
Тюкъ, тюкъ, гу - сель-цы,
Tiouc, tiouc, on chan-te doux
Pink, Pink, klin-ge Sai-te,
Scherzando (♩= 152)
(à Pointe d'arco)
62
arco
sul sol
Vl. I
arco
pizz.
Vl. II
pizz.
arco
pizz.
Vla.
Vlc.
arco
pizz.
Cb.
385

*) Pour l'instrument qui a le RÉ grave, exécuter:
Supprimez dans ce cas les parties des Violoncelle, Contrebasse et timbales du 63
Das Instrument mit dem tiefen d spielt:
In diesem Fall pausieren Violoncello, Kontrabaß und Pauken bei 63

*)
Cimb.
Timp.
B. I
-гу - ла, тюкъ, тюкъ... Да за-гу-ла, а дру-га - я
doux qu'ça!) Tiouc, tiouc, pour l'a-mour de vous, on la chant'tout
Fie-del _ Pink, Pink. Mi-sche dei-nen zar-ten Klang in
B. II
гу - ла Да за-гу-ла, а дру-га - я
doux qu'ça!) pour l'a-mour de vous, on la chant'tout
Fie-del _ Mi-sche dei-nen zar-ten Klang in
Vl. I
Vl. II
Vla.
Vlc.
sempre sim.
Cb.
sempre sim.
*)
Cimb.

64
395
Cimb.
Timp.
B. I
при - го - ва - ри - ва - ла: Тюкъ, тюкъ, гу__ сельцы,
bas; on la chan - te tout doux. Tiouc, tiouc, on la chan - te
uns' - ren lei - sen Ge - sang. Pink, Pink. Sach - te klin - ge,
B. II
при - го - ва - ри - ва - ла...
bas; on la chan - te tout doux.
uns' - ren lei - sen Ge - sang.
64
Vl. I
Vl. II
Vla.
Vlc.
f
Cb.
395
Cimb.

400
Cimb.
Timp.
Gr. C.
B. I
ба - ра - но - вы
tout doux, pour l'a
sacht, bis wir den
стру - ноч - ки...
- mour de vous...
schlauen Plan voll bracht.
Тюкъ, тюкъ...
Tiouc, tiouc...
Pink, Pink.
B. II
Уж ъ какъ
Où est
Ist Herr
Vl. I
Vl. II
Vla.
Vlc.
Cb.
400

Cimb.
simili
Timp.
simili
Gr. C.
B. I
Үжъ какъ до - ма ли ли - ca,
Où est ell'? est ell' chez ell'?
He, hol - la, ist er zu Haus?
B. II
до - ма ли ли - ca,
ell'? est - ell' chez ell'?
Rei - nek - ke zu Haus?
ужъ какъ
où est
He, hol -
pizz.
Vlc.
pizz.
Cb.
405
2. senza sord.
65
Cor. (Fa)
Cimb.
meno f
Timp.
Gr. C.
B. I
ужъ какъ до - ма ли ли - ca И -
où est - ell'? ma - dam' Re - nard est
Ist Herr Rei - nek - ke zu Haus, Herr
B. II
до - ма ли ли - ca,
ell'? est ell' chez ell'?
la, ist er zu Haus?
65
Vlc.
Cb.

*) pour l'instrument qui a le RÉ grave
fur das Instrument, welches das tiefe D hat

*) pour l'instrument qui a le RÉ grave
für das Instrument, welches das tiefe D hat

*) En cas que le Ré grave du Cimbalum manque remplacez le par la timbale
Wenn das Cimbalum kein tiefes D hat, soll es durch die Pauke ersetzt werden

425
Fg.
Cor. (Fa)
Tr. (Sib)
Cimb.
Timp.
Ptti.
(avec grelots)
T. de B.
(sans grelots)
(задорно)
(avec l'accent canaille)
B. I
чу - чел - ка,
Cor - ni - chon,
Oh - ne - herz?
Треть - я то По - дай - пи - ро - жокъ,
la troi - sièm', Mam'-sell' Tend - lu - Main,
O - der Fräu - lein Stehl - nicht - faul?
B. II
чу - чел - ка
Cor - ni - chon,
Oh - ne - herz?
Vl. I
Vl. II
Vla.
pizz.
Vlc.
pizz.
Cb.
425

68
Cimb.
Timp.
B. I
B. II
Vl. I
Vl. II
Vla.
Vlc.
А чет-вер-та-я Зажми-ку-ла-чекъ.
et la quat-ri-èm' Mam'sell' Fait-le-Poing.
O - der das Fräulein ken-ne-kei-nen Scherz?
Тюкъ, тюкъ,
Tiouc, tiouc...
Pink, Pink,
pizz.
a punta d'arco
gliss.
гу-сельцы = ба-ра-но-вы стру-ноч-ки...
on chan-te doux, un' jo-li-e chan-son pour vous...
klin-ge Sai-te, kling. Laß uns ein ar-tig Lie-del,
Тюкъ, тюкъ...
Tiouc, tiouc...
Pink, Pink,
430

*) come sopra

*) Come sopra voir 63

70
Cimb.
cuivrez
sim.
Timp.
Gr. C.
B. I
до - ма ли, да ужъ, какъ до - ма ли, да ужъ, какъ
ell', que fait elle, où est - ell', que fait elle, où est
Ant - wort wol - len wir, ja Ant - wort wol - len wir, stehn
B. II
до - ма ли, да ужъ, какъ до - ма ли, да ужъ, какъ
ell', que fait elle, où est - ell', que fait elle, où est
Ant - wort wol - len wir, ja Ant - wort wol - len wir, stehn
70
Vl. I
Vl. II
Vla.
pizz.
arco
Vlc.
molto
sim.
Cb.
440
Cimb.
p sub.
Timp.
subito p
p
B. I
до-ма ли ли - ca, Ужъ, какъ до-ма ли ли-ca И - ва-нов-на
elle et que fait elle, où est - ell', Ma-dam' Re-nard? peut - on la voir?
lang ge-nug da - hier, ist Herr - Rei-nek-ke zu Haus, Herr Rei-nek-ke?
subito p
B. II
до-ма ли ли - ca, Ужъ, какъ до-ма ли ли-ca И - ва-нов-на
elle et que fait elle, où est - ell', Ma-dam' Re-nard? peut - on la voir?
lang ge-nug da - hier, ist Herr - Rei-nek-ke zu Haus, Herr Rei-nek-ke?
pizz.
Vlc.
sub. p
Cb.
445
sub. p

71
Poco meno mosso ♩= 126
con sord.
Tr. (Si♭)
sfp
Cimb.
baguettes en bois
f
(Лиса высовываетъ кончикъ своего носа)
(Renard montre le bout de son nez)
(Der Fuchs läßt seine Nasenspitze sehen)
T. I
p
Кто тамъ пѣ - сни по -
Qu'est-c' que c'est qu'cett' chan -
Wer singt denn
B. II
71
Poco meno mosso ♩= 126
arco
(con sord.)
simili stacc.
Vl. I
sf p
(con sord.)
arco
Vl. II
sf p
stacc.
Cb.
450
(sim.)
Tr. (Si♭)
Cimb.
T. I
- етъ?
- son?
hier?
Да ужъ кто тамъ ли - ску зо -
qui est là et que m'veut -
Wer ruft nach
Vl. I
sfp
Vl. II
sfp
Cb.

455
72
Fg.
bouché
Cor.
(Fa)
bouché
Tr.
(Sib)
Cimb.
T. I
ветъ?
on?
mir?
B. I
И - дутъ звѣ - ри на пя - тахъ,
On est les bell's, les tout's bell's,
Hör' die Tie - re kom-men her
B. II
И - дутъ звѣ - ри на пя - тахъ,
On est les bell's, les tout's bell's,
Hör' die Tie - re kom-men her
72
Vl. I
Vl. II
Cb.
en glissant
le doigt)
455

Fg.
simili
Cor.
(Fa)
simili
Tr.
(Si♭)
fp
fp
B. I
Не - - сутъ ко - су на пле чахъ,
on est les bell's qui t'ap - pell'nt,
und voll Zorn sind sie gar sehr,
B. II
Не - - сутъ ко - су на - пле чахъ,
on est les bell's qui - t'ap - pell'nt,
und voll Zorn sind sie _ gar sehr,
Vl. I
f p
f p
Vl. II
fp
460
f p
Fg.
Cor.
(Fa)
Tr.
(Si♭)
fp
fp
B. I
Хо чутъ ли - сынь - ку по - сѣ - - чи
et c'qu'on a sous son man - teau,
wol - - len dich beim Kra - gen pak - - ken
B. II
Хо чутъ ли - сынь - ку - по - сѣ - - чи
et c'qu'on a sous son - man - teau,
wol - - - len dich beim Kra - gen pak - - ken
Vl. I
fp
f p
Vl. II
fp
f p

465 Molto rit. e pesante
a tempo
73
Fl. gr.
Ob.
Cl. (La)
Fg.
Cor. (Fa)
Tr. (Si♭)
Cimb.
Timp.
T. de B.
T. I
B. I
B. II
mf p e sempre sim.
Solo
ouvert
non f
(avec grelots)
(avec le pouce)
(Лиса въ ужасѣ)
(Renard épouvanté)
Der Fuchs, voll Schrecken)
(Звѣри машутъ косою)
(Les bêtes sortent le grand couteau)
(Die Tiere schwingen eine Sense)
Ахъ! вы — мо -
Ah! vous, — mes
Oh! sa - get
По са - мы - я пле - чи.
c'est un grand cou - teau.
und in Stük - ke hak - ken.
Molto rit. e pesante
a tempo
73
Vl. I
Vl. II
Vla.
Vlc.
Cb.
(senza sord.)
meno f
pizz.
sempre f
arco
465

470
Fl.gr.
Ob.
Fg.
9
1.
Cor.
(Fa)
Cimb.
T. I
и гла-зён-ки, гла - зён - ки И что вы мо- -
chers yeux, mes yeux qui ___ êt's deux, qu'a-vez - vous fait, ___
an, ihr mei-ne Al-ler-lieb-sten? was habt ihr ge- -
Vl.I
Vl.II
Vla.
Vlc.
sfp
sfp
sfp
Cb.
470

74
Fl. gr.
Ob.
Fg.
Cor. (Fa)
Cimb.
Timp.
mf (secco)
T. I
- и, милы - е дѣ - ла - ли?
— qu'a - vez - vous fait, mes yeux?
- tan, ihr mei - ne Al - ler - lieb - sten?
B. I
Мы смо - трѣ - ли, смо -
On a gui - gné, gui -
Lie - fen her, dich zu
B. II
Мы смо - трѣ - ли, смо -
On a gui - gné, gui -
Lie - fen her, dich zu
74
Vl. I
Vl. II
Vla.
Vlc.
sfp
arco
Cb.

*) Переходъ звука „ѣ" въ звукъ „у" внѣзапенъ. Звукъ „у" слѣдуетъ произносить въ губы, подражяя звуку низкой струны контрабаса.

75
480
Fl. gr.
Ob.
Cl. (La)
Solo
Fg.
Cor. (Fa)
Tr. (Sib)
Cimb.
Timp.
(avec le pouce)
T. de B.
(à grelots)
T. I
Ахъ, вы_ мо - и, но-жунь-ки,
Ah! vous mes pieds, si lé - gers
Ach sa - get nun, ihr mei - ne
B. I
-ли.
-ger.
schlit-zen.
B. II
-ли.
-ger.
schlit-zen.
75
Vl. I
meno f
Vl. II
meno f
pizz.
Vla.
pizz.
arco
Vlc.
come sopra
pizz.
Cb.
480

Fl.gr.
Ob.
Fg.
Cimb.
T. I
но - жунь - ки, и, что вы, мо - - и милы - я
à ___ cou - rir, qu'a - vez - vous fait, _ mes pieds, chers pieds,
Al - ler-treu'-sten, wie wollt ihr das _ tun, ihr mei - ne
Vl. I
Vl. II
Vla.
Vlc.
Cb.

76
485
Fl. gr.
Ob.
Fg.
f
Cimb.
Timp.
T. I
дѣ - ла - ли?
pour m'ser - vir?
Al - ler - treu - sten?
B. I
Мы бѣ - жа - ли, бѣ - - жа - - -
On a cou - ru tant qu'on a
Sto - ßen, krat - zen und bei - ßen,
B. II
Мы бѣ - жа - ли, бѣ - - жа - - -
On a cou - ru tant qu'on a
Sto - ßen, krat - zen und bei - ßen,
76
Vl I
Vl II
Vla.
Vlc.
arco
Cb.
485

Fl. gr.
Fg.
Cor. (Fa)
Tr. (Si♭)
Cimb.
Timp.
sans. grelots
T. d. B.
C. cl.
Trgl.
(Фальц)
(fausset)
*) (Falsett)
B. I
ли чтобъ звѣ - ри ли - ску не пор - ва (у)
pu, et les mé - chant's bêt' ne t'ont pas
daß die Bö - sen dich hier nicht zer - rei - - - -
B. II
ли чтобъ звѣ - ри ли - ску не пор - ва (у)
pu, et les mé chant's bêt' ne t'ont pas
daß die Bö - sen dich hier nicht zer - rei - - - -
pizz.
arco
Vl. I
Vl. II
Vla.
Vlc.
Cb.

*) какъ выше

77
490
Fl. gr.
Ob.
Cl. (La)
Fg.
Cor. (Fa)
Tr. (Sib)
Cimb.
Timp.
(avec le pouce)
T. d. B.
(a grelots)
T. I
A ——
Et ——
Ach mein
ты, мой хвостъ гля-ча росъ?
toi, et toi queue fri sée?
Schweif, mein schön-ge - kämm - ter!
B. I
-ли.
eue.
-ßen!
B. II
-ли.
eue.
-ßen!
77
Vl. I
Vl. II
pizz.
arco
etc. sim.
Vla.
pizz.
Vlc.
Cb.
490

495
78
Fl. gr.
Ob.
Cor. (Fa)
Tr. (Sib)
Cimb.
T. I
Чтобъ ли -
et les
Dann ist's
T. II
Я по пнямъ, по кус-тамъ,
à la haie m'suis ac - cro - chée,
Ist er noch so schön ge-kämmt,
B. I
По ко - ло-дамъ за-цѣп-лялъ Чтобъ ли -
hé - las! m'suis pris dans la haie, et les
wird er ein - mal fest-ge - klemmt. Dann ist's
B. II
Я по пнямъ, по кус-тамъ,
à la haie m'suis ac - cro - chée,
Ist er noch so schön ge-kämmt,
Vl. I
Vl. II
Vla.
Vlc.
arco
Cb.
arco

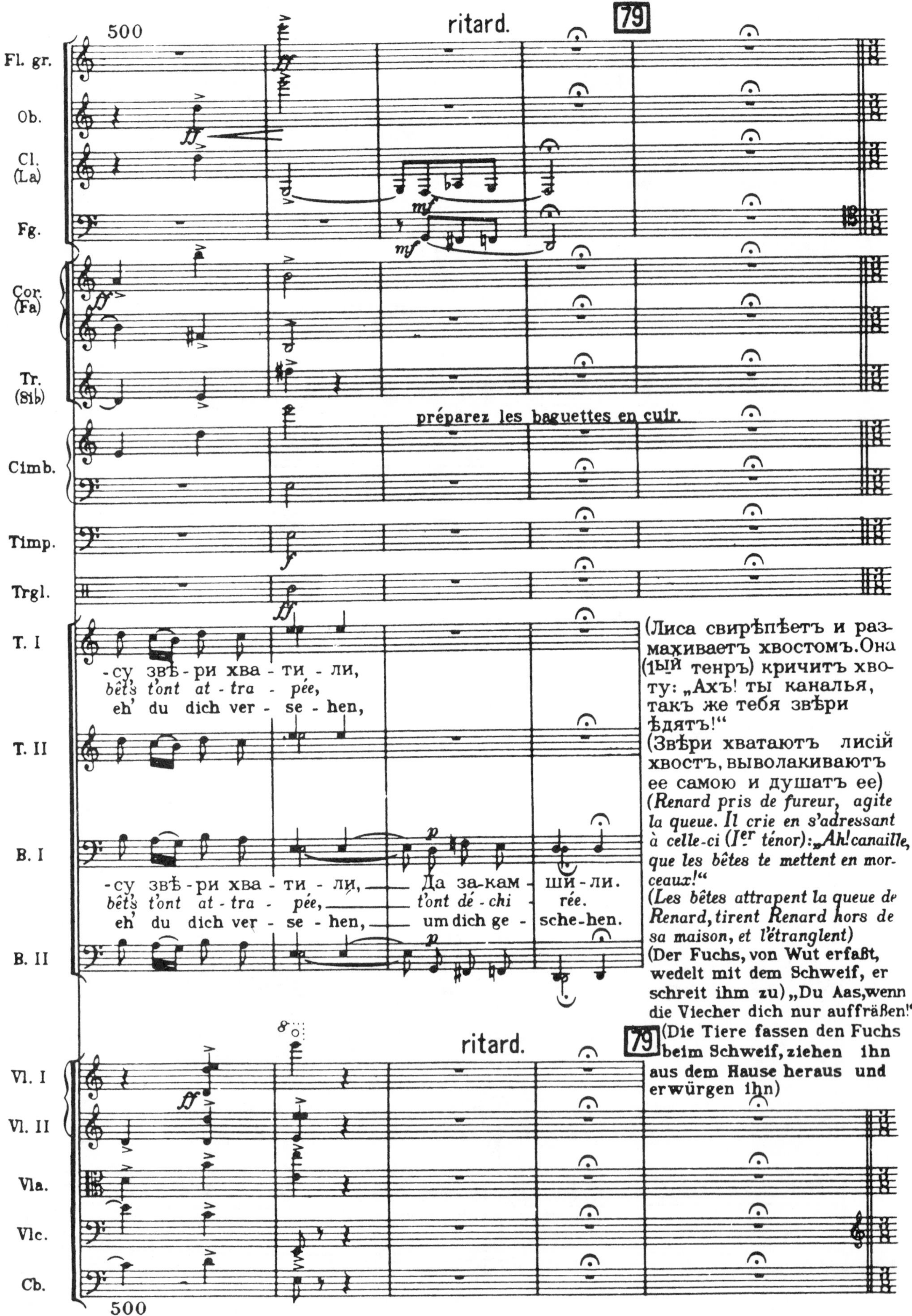
500
ritard.
79
Fl. gr.
Ob.
Cl. (La)
Fg.
Cor. (Fa)
Tr. (Sib)
préparez les baguettes en cuir.
Cimb.
Timp.
Trgl.
T. I
-су звѣ-ри хва-ти-ли,
bêt's t'ont at-tra-pée,
eh' du dich ver-se-hen,
T. II
B. I
-су звѣ-ри хва-ти-ли, Да за-кам-ши-ли.
bêt's t'ont at-tra-pée, t'ont dé-chi-rée.
eh' du dich ver-se-hen, um dich ge-sche-hen.
B. II
(Лиса свирѣпѣетъ и размахиваетъ хвостомъ. Она (1ый тенръ) кричитъ хвосту: „Ахъ! ты каналья, такъ же тебя звѣри ѣдятъ!"
(Звѣри хватаютъ лисій хвостъ, выволакиваютъ ее самою и душатъ ее)
(Renard pris de fureur, agite la queue. Il crie en s'adressant à celle-ci (Ier ténor): „Ah! canaille, que les bêtes te mettent en morceaux!"
(Les bêtes attrapent la queue de Renard, tirent Renard hors de sa maison, et l'étranglent)
(Der Fuchs, von Wut erfaßt, wedelt mit dem Schweif, er schreit ihm zu) „Du Aas, wenn die Viecher dich nur auffräßen!"
(Die Tiere fassen den Fuchs beim Schweif, ziehen ihn aus dem Hause heraus und erwürgen ihn)
ritard.
79
Vl. I
Vl. II
Vla.
Vlc.
Cb.
500

80 Vivo ♩.=84
505
Fl. gr.
Ob.
Cl. (La)
Fg.
Cor. (Fa)
Tr. (Sib)
Cimb.
(Оба тенора и оба баса вопятъ благимъ матомъ) Лиса издыхаетъ
(Les deux ténors et les deux basses hurlent de toutes leurs forces) Renard expire
(Beide Tenöre und beide Bässe heulen mit voller Kraft.) Der Fuchs stirbt.
T. I
A
T. II
B. I
A
B. II
80 Vivo ♩.=84
Vl. I
Vl. II
Vla
Vlc.
Cb.
505

*) Ces notes mises entre parenthèse se jouent seulement au cas où le Cimbalum ne possède pas le ré grave.
Die Noten in Klammern werden nur dann gespielt, wenn das Cymbal kein tiefes d hat

Fg.
Cimb.
Timp.
T. I
T. II
B. I
Vlc.
Cb.
А ти-
qui n'peut
un-er-
Я бо-я-лась ти-пу-на,
C'est que j'ai mon p'tit commerc',
Ahn-test nicht wo-her dir droht,
-ча долго не жи-ла?
quoi nous quit-ter dé-jà?
liegst du nun als To-ter!
arco
pizz.
515
-пунъ то не судь-я,
pas s'pas-ser de moi.
-war-tet schnell der Tod.
А судь-я то ла-ды-га.
Jean Lou-is tap'-sur sa femm',
Al-le Tie-re vol-ler

82
520
Cimb.
T. I
Ла-ды-ги-ны дѣ - ти
ell' tap' sur son ma - t'las,
daß zu End' die
Хо-тятъ у-ле-тѣ - ти
ils crient, les chiens a - boient,
bö-se Zeit, voll von
B. I
Freud',
82
pizz.
Vl. I
Vl. II
Vla.
Vlc.
sempre sim.
arco
sempre sim.
Cb.
520

Ob.
Cl. (La)
Cor. (Fa)
Cimb.
T. I
T. II
B. I
B. II
Vl. I
Vl. II
Vla.
Vlc.
Cb.
mf
près du chevalet
хо-тятъ у - ле - тѣ - ти.
leurs en - fants sont au bois.
Angst, Be - schwer und Leid,
За и - ва - новъ го -
Ils ont dit à Re -
Bel - len, pfei - fen, mi -
pizz.

Fl. gr.
Cl. (La)
Fg.
Cor. (Fa)
Tr. (Sib)
Cimb.
Timp.
T. I
T. II
B. I
B. II
Vl. I
Vl. II
Vla.
Vlc.
Cb.
poco sf
f>p
arco
родъ
nard:
au - en.
О - ни...
„Eh,...
Weit...
О - ни по гра-мот-кѣ пи - шутъ,
„Eh, Re-nard, vien-dras-tu pas?
Weit und breit durch Feld und Au - en.
Да на...
t'au - ras...
Bel - len...
Да на ли-си-цу ды - шутъ.
t'au-ras du cho-co - lat"...
Bel - len, pfei-fen, mi - au - en.

83
Fg.
Cimb.
Timp.
B. I
Лисынька, лисица
Поди поводицу
Renard a dit: „Ça va"
Sur la plac' du village,
Reinekke, du Roter,
steh doch auf, du Toter.
Vlc.
Cb.
525
pizz.
Fg.
Cimb.
Timp
B. I
На дорогѣ волки
Горохъ молото-
les loups battaient les pois;
Renard se dé-
Willst du nicht den Wölfen
Erbsen dreschen
arco
Cb.
530

84
Fl. gr.
Ob.
sim.
Cl. (La)
sim.
Fg.
sim.
Cor. (Fa)
Tr. (Sib)
Cimb.
Ptti. Gr. C.
Trgl.
B. I
-ти-ли. Лис-ки-ны ре-бя-та Лис-кѣ то ска-
-rang' pas. Re-nard est sur le poêl! Gar', Re-nard, les
hel-fen, Rei-nek-ke am O-fen liegt, wie er das zu
arco
84
Vl. I
meno f
pizz.
Vl. II
meno f
pizz.
Vla.
Vlc.
Cb.

Fl. gr.
Fg.
Cimb.
B. I
-за - ли, Лисынь-ка то съ пе - чи об - ло - ма - ла
voi - là!" Il a sau - té par terr', il s'est cas - sé le
hö - ren kriegt, wird er mun - ter, springt her - un - ter, brichtein
Cb.
535
85
Cimb.
Timp.
T. I
Сёмъ, сёмъ, сёмъ, пе - ре - сёмъ, пе - ре - сёмъ, на ло -
Zoum! zoum! zoum! pa - ta - zoum pa - ta - zoum c'est tant
Dum, dum, dum, di - del - dum, di - del - dum, sehr zum
T. II
Сёмъ, сёмъ, сёмъ, пе - ре - сёмъ, пе - ре - сёмъ, на ло -
Zoum! zoum! zoum! pa - ta - zoum pa - ta - zoum c'est tant
Dum, dum, dum, di - del - dum, di - del - dum, sehr zum
B. I
пле - чи
bras...
Bein.
85
Vl. I
Vl. II
arco
stacc.
Vla.
arco
stacc.
Vlc.
pizz.
arco
Cb.

540
Cimb.
Timp.
T. I
пат - кѣ ис - пе - ченъ.
mieux pour les poul's.
Glück für Gok - ke - lein.
Сёмъ, сёмъ,
Zoum! zoum!
Dum, dum,
T. II
пат - кѣ ис - пе - ченъ.
mieux pour les poul's.
Glück für Gok - ke - lein.
Сёмъ, сёмъ,
Zoum! zoum!
Dum, dum,
B. I
Et
Му - жикъ пѣс - ню спѣ - (в)лъ...
c'est ain si qu'on di - it...
Nun ge - nug ge - sun - gen...
Vl. I
Vl. II
Vla.
pizz.
Vlc.
arco
pizz.
Cb.
540

Fl. gr.
Cimb.
sf
T. I
сёмъ пе - ре - семъ
zoum! pa - ta - zoum!
dum, di - del - dum!
T. II
сёмъ пе - ре - семъ
zoum! pa - ta - zoum!
dum, dì - del - dum!
B. I
На ка - пуст - никъ сѣ - (ѣ)лъ
que l'hi - stoir' fi - nit.
Und ge - tanzt, ge - sprun - gen.
Vl. I
Vl. II
sf
Vla.
sf
pizz.
Vlc.
arco
(arco)
Cb.

86
545
Fl. gr.
Cimb.
Timp.
T. I
Сёмъ,сёмъ,семъ, пе-ресёмъ, пе-ре-сёмъ пе-ресемъ, пе-ресемъ
Zoum zoum zoum pa-ta-zoum! pa-ta-zoum! pa-ta-zoum! pa-ta-zoum!
Dum, dum, dum, di-del-dum, di-del-dum, di-del-dum, di-del-dum.
T. II
Сёмъ,сёмъ,семъ, пе-ресёмъ, пе-ре-сёмъ пе-ресемъ, пе-ресемъ,Съѣлъ три
Zoum! zoum! zoum! pa-ta-zoum! pa-ta-zoum! pa-ta-zoum! pa-ta-zoum! A pré
Dum, dum, dum, di-del-dum, di-del-dum, di-del-dum, di-del-dum. Hört, ich
B. I
86
Vl. I
Vl. II
stacc.
Vla.
arco
Vlc.
pizz.
arco
Cb.
545

Fl. gr.
Cimb.
T. I
Три кос - тра пи - ро - говъ
ous qu'y au - ra d'quoi man - ger,
Lie - ber wä - re mir Wein!
T. II
ко - ро - ба бли новъ,
sent on va al - ler,
möch - te jetzt ein Bier!
За -
et
Der
Vl. I
Vl. II
stacc.
Vla.
Vlc.
Cb.

550

Fl. gr.
Cimb.
T. I
За - ходъ - ка - ла - чей, Ма -
On i - ra ous qu'y au-ra des
Soll mir Bier auch recht sein! S'ist
T. II
у локъ ро - гу - лекъ
ous qu'y au - ra d'quoi boir!
ist nicht gut da - hier!
Ма -
des
S'ist
Vl. I
Vl. II
Vla.
Vlc.
Cb.

550

Fl. gr.
Cimb.
T. I
-кин - ни-цу съ суло-ю,
beaux bei-gnets à l'huil' d'noix,
bes - ser zu ver-tra-gen
О - винъ ки-се-ля,
et puis plein un ton
auf lee-rem Ma-gen,
T. II
-кин - ни-цу съ суло-ю,
beaux bei-gnets à l'huil' d'noix,
bes - ser zu ver-tra-gen
О - винъ ки-се-ля,
et puis plein un ton
auf lee-rem Ma-gen.
B. I
О - винъ ки-се-ля,
et puis plein un ton
auf lee-rem Ma-gen,
Vl. I
Vl. II
Vla.
Vlc.
Cb.

87
555
Fl. gr.
Cimb.
Timp.
T. I
По ва-рей-ку щей.
neau d'bon vin nou-veau.
hört' ich sa-gen.
T. II
По ва-рей-ку щей.
neau d'bon vin nou-veau.
hört' ich sa-gen.
B. I
По ва-рей-ку щей.
neau d'bon vin nou-veau.
hört' ich sa-gen.
Гос-по-ди по-ми-луй, На
Sei-gneur, par-don-nez-nous! Sur
Herr Gott, sei uns gnä-dig, wir
B. II
По ва-рей-ку щей.
...d'bon vin nou-veau.
hört' ich sa-gen.
87
Vl. I
Vl. II
Vla.
Vlc.
Cb.
555
pizz.

Fg.
Cimb.
Timp.
B. I
ко - ни - кѣ Да - ни - ло На лав - кѣ Флоръ На
sa bête est Jean Ba - doux, sur l'homm' sa têt', dans
sind noch al - le le - dig, gib mir ein Weib, daß
Vl. I
Vl. II
Vla.
Vlc.
Cb.
arco
pizz.

88
560
Fl. gr.
Ob.
Cl. (La)
Fg.
Cor. (Fa)
Tr. (Sib)
Cimb.
Timp.
Pttі. e Gr. C.
Trgl.
T. I
Въпе-чи ка - ла - чи,
et voi-là qu'il pleut,
Den fri-schen Ku - chen
T. II
Въпе-чи ка - ла - чи,
et voi-là qu'il pleut,
Den fri-schen Ku - chen
B. I
пе-чи при-го - воръ. Въпе-чи ка - ла - чи,
sa_têt' rien du tout; et voi-là qu'il pleut,
ich's nicht e - wig bleib'. Den fri-schen Ku - chen
Vl. I
Vl. II
pizz.
pizz.
Vla.
Vlc.
Cb.
arco

565
Fl. gr.
Ob.
Cl. (La)
Fg.
Cor. (Fa)
Tr. (Sib)
Cimb.
Timp.
Pttl. e Gr. C.
Trgl.
T. I
Какъ о - гонь го - ря - чи
on a fait un bon feu
möcht ich gern ver - su - chen.
T. II
Какъ о - гонь го - ря - чи
on a fait un bon feu
möcht ich gern ver - su - chen.
B. I
Какъ о - гонь го - ря - чи Про бо - ярь пе - че -
on a fait un bon feu en l'hon - neur d'nos mes -
möcht ich gern ver - su - chen. Doch der_ ist für die
Vl. I
Vl. II
Vla.
Vlc.
Cb.
565

89
Fl. gr.
Ob.
Cl. (La)
Fg.
Cor. (Fa)
Tr. (Si♭)
Cimb.
Timp.
Ptti. e Gr. C.
Trgl.
T. I
На ѣ - ха - ли бо - я - ре да со -
nos mes - sieurs sont ar - ri - vés, leurs chiens
Die kom - men hoch zu Wa - gen an - ge -
T. II
На ѣ - ха - ли бо - я - ре да со -
nos mes - sieurs sont ar - ri - vés, leurs chiens
Die kom - men hoch zu Wa - gen an - ge -
B. I
ны. На ѣ - ха - ли бо - я - ре да со -
sieurs: nos mes - sieurs sont ar - ri - vés, leurs chiens
Herrn. Die kom - men hoch zu Wa - gen an - ge -
B. II
На ѣ - ха - ли бо - я - ре да со -
nos mes - sieurs sont ar - ri - vés, leurs chiens
Die kom - men hoch zu Wa - gen an - ge -
89
Vl. I
Vl. II
Vla.
Vlc.
Cb.

570
Fl.gr.
Ob.
Cl. (La)
p
Fg.
Cor. (Fa)
Tr. (Sib)
Cimb.
Timp.
Ptti.e Gr. C.
Trgl.
T. I
бакъ на вез - ли,
ont, fait cou - cher,
fahr'n zum Ja - gen.
T. II
бакъ на вез - ли,
ont, fait cou - cher,
fahr'n zum Ja - gen.
B. I
бакъ на вез - ли, Со - ба - ки то взду - ри - ли Да -
ont fait cou - cher, leurs chiens se sont fâ - chés, Re -
fahr'n zum Ja - gen. Die Hun - de bel - len_ laut, Fuchs
B. II
бакъ на вез - ли, Со - ба - ки то взду - ри - ли Да -
ont fait cou - cher, leurs chiens se sont fâ - chés, Re -
fahr'n zum Ja - gen. Die Hun - de bel - len_ laut, Fuchs
Vl. I
Vl. II
Vla.
Vlc.
Cb.
570
pizz.

90
Cl. (La)
Fg.
Cimb.
Timp.
mf
(glissando pour timbale à levier)
T. I
f
(говоромъ) Вотъ вамъ сказ-ка! а мнѣ крин-ка мас-ла.
(parle) Et si l'hi-stoir'vous a plu, pay ez moic'qui m'est dû
(gespr.) Un-ser Lohn, bit - te,wenn's ge-fiel!
T. II
(говоромъ) Вотъ вамъ сказ-ка!
B. I
f (говоромъ)
лиску у - ку - си-ли.. Вотъвамъ сказ-ка!
-nard a em - po - ché.. (gespr.)
wehr'dich dei - ner_ Haut! Aus ist das Spiel!
B. II
f (говоромъ)
лиску у - ку - си-ли.. Вотъвамъ сказ-ка!
-nard a em - po - ché.. (gespr.)
wehr'dich dei - ner_ Haut! Aus ist das Spiel!
90
pizz.
Vl. I
arco salt.
Vl. II
arco salt.
Vla.
f
Vlc.
f
gliss.
Cb.
gliss.
arco
Enchaîner

MARCHE [MARCH]

Departure of the Actors

11
Fg.
Cor. (Fa)
Tr. (La)
Ptti. e Gr. C.
10
15
fff
20

To Madame Eugenia Errazuriz

Ragtime

for Eleven Instruments

(1918)

Pablo Picasso's cover design for the first edition (1919)
of Stravinsky's piano arrangement of *Ragtime*

Note

The composition of *Histoire du soldat* by no means exhausted Stravinsky's interest in jazz. On the contrary, being fascinated 'by its truly popular appeal, its freshness and the novel rhythm which so clearly revealed its negro origin' [the composer's words], he decided to idealize this new dance music in the form of a concert piece, and accordingly wrote a *Ragtime* for eleven players. Not unnaturally, the work is fairly close to *Histoire* in style; but jazz influences twist its melodic line into even more sinuous chromaticisms and—a remarkable thing in his works of this period—the common time signature is unchanged throughout its 178 bars.

The first sketches were completed on 27 November 1917, with a full draft finished on 5 March 1918. This first version required a piano in addition to the cimbalom. Jean Hugo—painter, designer, and intimate of the Cocteau-Picasso circle—recalled Stravinsky's private piano performance of 'a ragtime that he had just composed' for an audience of Picasso, Ballets Russes impresario Sergey Diaghilev, the great dancer-choreographer Léonide Massine,* and composers Georges Auric and Francis Poulenc. It is probable that the piece was Stravinsky's piano reduction of *Ragtime.* (Picasso's cover for the first edition of this version—published in 1919 by Editions de la Sirène—is reproduced on the facing page.)

Ragtime was dedicated to the Chilean Eugenia Errazuriz. A generous patron of both Stravinsky and Picasso, it was she who brought the two artists together, arranging for their first meeting, in Rome. The composer's indebtedness to her included commissions for the *Etude* for pianola (1917) and *Piano-Rag-Music* (1919), as well as for a monthly stipend of a thousand francs, sent to Stravinsky from 1916 until the end of the war.

*Some years later, *Ragtime* was produced by Massine at Covent Garden as a dance *divertissement* for himself and Lydia Lopokova.

INSTRUMENTATION

[strictly, eleven *players*]

Flute [Grande Flûte, Fl.]

Clarinet in A [Clarinette en La, Cl.]

Horn in F [Cor en Fa, Cor.]

Cornet in B♭ [Cornet à Piston en Si♭, C. à P.]

Trombone [Trombone, Tr^{ne}]

Percussion

- Snare Drum *with snares on* [Caisse claire à corde , C.cl. à c.]
- Snare Drum *with snares off* [Caisse claire sans corde , C.cl.s.c.]
- Large Drum [Grande Caisse, Gr.C.]
- Suspended Cymbal [Cymbale, Cymb.]

Cimbalom* [Cymbalum, Cymb^{m}]

Solo strings:

1st Violin [1er Violon, Vl. I]

2nd Violin [2e Violon, Vl. II]

Viola [Alto]

Bass [Contrebasse, C,B.]

*See the footnote, p. 22, for a description of this instrument and its performance techniques.

M.M. ♩ = 160
Grande Flûte
Clarinette en La
Cor en Fa
Cornet à Pistons en Sib
Trombone
baguettes en bois
trem.
Caisse claire à corde
Caisse claire sans corde
Grande Caisse
Cymbale
un seul exécutant
préparez vite la baguette à tête en capoc
Cymbalum
meno f sub.
M.M. ♩ = 160
1er Violon
2e Violon
Alto
Contrebasse
gliss.
pizz.
arco

1
5
Fl.
Cl.
Cor.
simile
solo
C.à P.
C.cl.s.c.
baguette à tête en capoc
Gr.C.
Cymb^m
sub.f
arco
Vl.I
subito f
pizz.
Vl.II
Alto
C.B.

2
10
15
Fl.
Cl.
Cor.
C.à P.
Tr.ne
C.cl.s.c.
Gr.C.
Cymb.
Cymbm.
Vl.I
Vl.II
Alto
C.B.
meno f
poco sf
poco meno f
subito f
mailloche
bag. en capoc
étouffez
Ped.
secco
pizz.
arco
sub. p

3
solo
Fl.
Cl.
Cor.
mf
Cymb^m.
cuivré-tout près du chevalet
non arpegg.
pizz.
arco
Vl. I
tres sec
sf
avec doigts
Vl. II
pizz.
Alto
C.B.
20
4
C. à P.
con sord.
simile
ordinairement
du talon
molto
Sim.
sfp

5
Fl.
Cl.
Cor.
Tr.ne
bag. en bois
C.cl.à c.
Cymbm
avec toute la longueur de l'archet
tout l'archet
Vl. I
sul Re
Vl. II
Alto
C.B.
più f
meno f
25
6
C.à P.
senza sord.
poco sf > pp
arpegg. rapido
sub. meno f
très court et mordant
cresc.
pizz.
arco
secco
poco sf
30

7
8
35
Cl.
meno f
Cor.
sf
f
C.à P.
sub. meno f
Tr.ne
C.cl.s.c.
poco
Gr.C.
bag. en capoc.
Cymbm
sub. meno f
très sec
Vl. I
pizz.
Vl. II
pizz.
mf
arco
Alto
Alto
C.B.

9
40
très sec
Fl.
Cl.
très sec
Cor.
très sec
C. à P.
Tr.ne
bag. en bois
C.cl.à c.
C.cl.s.c.
bag. en capoc
poco sf
Gr. C.
mailloche
mailloche
Cymb.m
secco
arco
tranquillo
pizz.
arco
du talon
Vl. I
Vl. II
Alto
C.B.
pizz.
arco
40
9

10
45
Fl.
Cl.
Cor.
C. a P.
C.cl.s.c.
Gr.C.
Cymbm.
Vl. I
Vl. II
Alto
C. B.
sf
mf
poco sf
bag. en caoutc.
ff
mailloche
p
pizz.
arco
sim.
f

11
50
Fl.
Cl.
Cor.
C. à P.
Tr.ne
C. cl. à c.
Cymbm.
Vl. I
Vl. II
Alto
C. B.
bouché
poco sfp simile
détaché
con sord.
gliss.
bag. en bois
m.d.
m.g.
p sempre
sul sol
pizz.
arco
sub. p

12
55
Fl.
sff
Cl.
sff
Cor.
p
C. à P.
sf
Tr.ne
p
Cymb.m
sf
m.d. p
m.d.
Vl. I
arco
pizz.
p
più f
sf
Vl. II
arco
pizz.
mp
Alto
C. B.

13
60
Fl.
mp
Cl.
mp
ouvert
Cor.
p
C. à P.
Tr.ne
Cymbm.
m.d.
pizz.
Vl. I
mf
pizz.
Vl. II
mf
pizz.
Alto
mf
C. B.
60
13

14
65
Fl.
Cl.
Cor.
C. à P.
Tr.ne
Gr. C.
Cymb.m
Vl. I
Vl. II
Alto
C. B.
senza sord.
mailloche
molto
m.d.
p sempre
arco
pizz.
65
14

15
70
Fl.
Cl.
Cor.
C. à P.
Tr.ne
bag. en cap.
sec
C.cl.s.c.
mailloche
Gr. C.
Cymbm.
Vl. I
arco
Vl. II
arco
Alto
C. B.
70
15

16
solo
C. à P.
(rapido)
Cymbm.
pizz.
arco
Vl. I
Vl. II
Alto
C. B.
mf
p
75
16
17
Fl.
Cl.
Cor.
C. à P.
Tr.ne
Gr. C.
Cymbm.
(senza Ped.)
Vl. I
Vl. II
Alto
C. B.
80
17

18
Fl.
Cl.
solo
mf
sf
Cymb^m.
sul Sol
arco
Vl. I
Vl. II
Alto
f
p
19
Gr. C.
pizz.
non arpegg.
avec
2 doigts
fp
C. B.
85

20
Cor.
C.à P.
Tr.ne
solo
gliss.
Vl. I
Vl. II
Alto
C. B.
arco
90 stacc.
20
21
Cor.
C.à P.
C.cl.s.c.
Gr.C.
sempre mf
Cymbm.
21
sul Sol
pizz.
Vl. I
Vl. II
Alto
C. B.
95
*) Les queues en bas - m.g. avec la mailloche
Les queues en haut - m.d. bag. en capoc

22
100
23
Fl.
Cl.
Cor.
C. à P.
C.cl.s.c.
Gr. C.
Cymbm.
Vl. I
Vl. II
Alto
C. B.
sf
mf
sub meno f
sul Sol
arco
pizz.
sff
mf sub.

24
105
Fl.
Cl.
Cor.
C. à P.
Tr.ne
C.cl.à c.
Cymbm.
Vl. I
Vl. II
Alto
C. B.
meno f
pp
détaché
gliss.
bag. en bois
ossia
pour l'instrument
qui a le Re grave
arco

25
110
Fl.
Cl.
Cor.
C. à P.
solo
Tr.ne
marcato
Gr. C.
p
Cymbm.
sf
près du chevalet
ordinairement
Vl. I
non arpeggiato
f
sf
Vl. II
pizz.
arco
pizz.
Alto
pizz.
arco
pizz.
C. B.
pizz.
p
molto
110
25

26
Fl.
Cl.
Cor.
C.à P.
solo
Tr.ne
mf
molto
Gr. C.
Cymbm.
sul Sol
Vl.I
sfp
mf
arco
sul Sol
Vl.II
arco
Alto
arco
C. B.
p
26 115
27
solo
Cl.
sub.
Cor.
p
bag. en capoc
C.cl.s.c.
bag. en capoc
Gr. C.
Cymbm.
pizz.
C. B.
27
120

125
28
Fl.
Cl.
solo
f très détaché
Cor.
C. cl.s.c.
Gr. C.
p
Cymb.
ordinairement
Cymb^m.
Vl. I
f
Vl. II
f
Alto
f
arco
C. B.
125
28

Fl.
Cl.
solo
en dehors
mf
Cor.
poco
p
C. à P.
[soli-très en dehors
Tr.ne
Gr. C.
Cymb.
Cymb.m
f
laissez vibrer
étouffez
Vl. I
pizz.
C. B.
130
29
Fl.
Cor.
pp
C. cl. s. c.
Cymb.
Cymb.m
meno f
Vl. I
Vl. II
pizz.
Alto
pizz.
C. B.
pizz.
29

30
135
Fl.
Cl.
Cor.
C. à P.
Tr.ne
C. cl. s. c.
Gr. C.
Cymb.
Cymb.m
Vl. I
Vl. II
Alto
C. B.
sub. f
ff
solo
f
poco meno f
sub. f
mf
bag. en capoc
f
étouffez
sub. f
étouffez
ff
arco
pizz.
p sub.
arco
arco
ff
I
II
arco
pizz.
p sub.
arco
arco
pizz.
f
p sub.
arco
ff
135
30

140
31
Fl.
meno f
Cl.
meno f
Cor.
poco
C. à P.
Tr.ne
mailloche
Gr. C.
Cymb.m
meno f
Ped.
ff
secco
sf
Vl. I
pizz.
arco
solo
p
sf
mf
Vl. II
arco
pizz.
f
Alto
pizz.
arco
p
sf
p
f
C. B.
arco
pizz.
ff
mf
140
31

Fl.
Cl.
Cor.
Cymb.m
Vl. I
Vl. II
Alto
C.B.
solo
solo
cuivré-tout près du chevalet
très sec
non arpegg.
pizz.
avec 2 doigts
arco
145
32
simile
ordinairement
secco
molto
sim.
du talon
non arpegg.
pizz.

33
150
Fl.
Cl.
Cor.
con sord.
C. à P.
Tr. ne
bag. en bois.
C. cl. à c.
Cymb.m
avec toute la longueur de l'archet
tout l'archet
Vl. I
sul Re
Vl. II
Alto
pizz.
C. B.
piu f
meno f
150
33

34
155
Fl.
Cl.
Cor.
poco sf pp
senza sord.
C.à P.
poco sf pp
Tr.ne
C.cl.à c.
arpegg. rapido
Cymbm.
sub. meno f
mf cresc.
Vl. I
très court et mordant
f cresc.
Vl. II
pizz.
arco
Alto
C. B.
poco sf secco

35
160
Cl.
Cor.
C. à P.
Tr.ne
C.cl.s.c.
Gr. C.
Cymb.m
Vl. I
Vl. II
Alto
C. B.
mf
sf
bag. en capoc
poco
sub. meno
très sec
très court et mordant
cresc.
arco
secco
160
35

36
165
Fl.
Cl.
meno f
Cor.
meno f
C.à P.
sub. meno
Tr.ne
C.cl.à c.
bag. en bois
Gr. C.
mailloche
Cymbm.
sub. meno f
Vl. I
pizz.
arco
Vl. II
pizz.
arco
Alto
pizz.
C. B.
pizz.
sub. meno
arco
pizz.
arco
ma secco
165
36

37
très sec
Fl.
Cl.
Cor.
C. à P.
bag. en capoc
C. cl. s. c.
mailloche
Gr. C.
secco
Cymb^m.
pizz.
arco
du talon
Vl. I
tranquillo
sim.
Vl. II
Alto
C. B.
poco sf
secco
37

38
170
Fl.
sub. meno
più f
Cl.
sub. meno
Cor.
C. à P.
bag. en capoc
C.cl.s.c.
mailloche
Gr. C.
Cymbm.
pizz.
arco
Vl. I
Vl. II
Alto
C. B.
170
38

END OF EDITION

DOVER OPERA AND CHORAL SCORES

Christmas Oratorio in Full Score, Johann Sebastian Bach. (27230-3) $16.95

Eleven Great Cantatas, J. S. Bach. (23268-9) $17.95

Magnificat in D and the Six Motets in Full Score, Johann Sebastian Bach. (28804-8) $14.95

Mass in B Minor in Full Score, Johann Sebastian Bach. (25992-7) $15.95

St. John Passion in Full Score, Johann Sebastian Bach. (27755-0) $11.95

Seven Great Sacred Cantatas in Full Score, Johann Sebastian Bach. (24950-6) $14.95

Six Great Secular Cantatas in Full Score, Johann Sebastian Bach. (23934-9) $17.95

Fidelio in Full Score, Ludwig van Beethoven. (24740-6) $14.95

Missa Solemnis in Full Score, Ludwig van Beethoven. (26894-2) $17.95

Norma in Full Score, Vincenzo Bellini. (27970-7) $24.95

L'Enfance de Christ, Op. 25, in Full Score: Sacred Trilogy for Solo Voices, Chorus and Orchestra, Hector Berlioz. (40852-3) $15.95

Carmen in Full Score, Georges Bizet. (25820-3) $24.95

Alto Rhapsody, Song of Destiny, Nänie and Song of the Fates in Full Score, Johannes Brahms. (28528-6) $12.95

German Requiem in Full Score, Johannes Brahms. (25486-0) $12.95

Pelleas et Melisande in Full Score, Claude Debussy. (Available in U.S. only.) (24825-9) $23.95

Lucia Di Lammermoor in Full Score, Gaetano Donizetti. (27113-7) $23.95

Requiem in Full Score, Gabriel Fauré. (Not available in France or Germany.) (27155-2) $10.95

Orfeo ed Euridice in Full Score, Christoph Willibald Gluck. (27324-5) $12.95

Faust in Full Score, Charles Gounod. (28349-6) $29.95

Four Coronation Anthems in Full Score, George Frideric Handel. (40627-X) $12.95

Judas Maccabaeus in Full Score, George Frideric Handel. (29691-1) $14.95

The Messiah in Full Score, George Frideric Handel. (26067-4) $12.95

The Creation in Full Score, Joseph Haydn. (26411-4) $14.95

"Nelson" Mass and Mass in Time of War in Full Score, Joseph Haydn. (28108-6) $14.95

Hansel and Gretel in Full Score, Engelbert Humperdinck. (28818-8) $19.95

Pagliacci in Full Score, Ruggiero Leoncavallo. (27363-6) $19.95

Cavalleria Rusticana in Full Score, Pietro Mascagni. (Available in U.S. only.) (27866-2) $12.95

Elijah in Full Score, Felix Mendelssohn. (28504-9) $18.95

Les Préludes and Other Symphonic Poems in Full Score, Franz Liszt. (28322-4) $15.95

Symphonies Nos. 5 & 6 in Full Score, Gustav Mahler. (26888-8) $24.95

Symphony No. 7 in Full Score, Gustav Mahler. (27339-3) $13.95

Symphony No. 9 in Full Score, Gustav Mahler. (27492-6) $11.95

Major Orchestral Works, Felix Mendelssohn. (23184-4) $19.95

Symphony No. 5 ("Reformation") in Full Score, Felix Mendelssohn. (27875-1) $9.95

Complete Serenades in Full Score, Series I, Wolfgang A. Mozart. (26565-X) $15.95

Complete Serenades in Full Score, Series II, Wolfgang A. Mozart. (26566-8) $12.95

Concerti for Wind Instruments in Full Score, Wolfgang A. Mozart. (25228-0) $15.95

Later Symphonies: Full Scores to Symphonies 35 to 41, Wolfgang Amadeus Mozart. (23052-X) $14.95

Piano Concertos, Nos. 17–22 in Full Score, Wolfgang Amadeus Mozart. (23599-8) $18.95

Piano Concertos, Nos. 23–27 in Full Score, Wolfgang Amadeus Mozart. (23600-5) $16.95

Piano Concerto No. 26 in D Major ("Coronation"), K.537; The Autograph Score, Wolfgang A. Mozart. (26747-4) $12.95

17 Divertimenti for Various Instruments, Wolfgang A. Mozart. (23862-8) $13.95

Symphony No. 2 in E Minor, Op. 27, in Full Score, Serge Rachmaninoff. (Available in U.S. only.) (40629-6) $15.95

Scheherazade in Full Score, Nikolay Rimsky-Korsakov. (24734-1) $12.95

Four Symphonies in Full Score, Franz Schubert. (23681-1) $14.95

Great Works for Piano and Orchestra in Full Score, Robert Schumann. (24340-0) $10.95

Great Romantic Cello Concertos in Full Score, Robert Schumann, Camille Saint-Saëns, Antonin Dvořák. (24584-5) $11.95

Petrushka in Full Score (Original Version), Igor Stravinsky. (Available in U.S. only.) (25680-4) $11.95

Nutcracker Suite in Full Score, Peter Ilyitch Tchaikovsky. (25379-1) $9.95

L'Estro Armonico, Op. 3, in Full Score: 12 Concertos for 1, 2 and 4 Violins, Antonio Vivaldi. (40631-8) $14.95

Paperbound unless otherwise indicated. Prices subject to change without notice. Available at your book dealer or write for free catalogues to Dept. 23, Dover Publications, Inc., 31 East 2nd Street, Mineola, N.Y. 11501. Please indicate field of interest. Each year Dover publishes over 200 books on fine art, music, crafts and needlework, antiques, languages, literature, children's books, chess, cookery, nature, anthropology, science, mathematics, and other areas.

Manufactured in the U.S.A.